THE MAGIC OF
THE AURA

Best Wishes

Billy Roberts

THE MAGIC OF THE AURA

Billy Roberts

APEX PUBLISHING LTD

First published in 2008 by
Apex Publishing Ltd
PO Box 7086, Clacton on Sea, Essex, CO15 5WN, England

www.apexpublishing.co.uk

British Library Cataloguing-in-Publication Data
A catalogue record for this book
is available from the British Library

ISBN 1-904444-93-8   978-1-904444-93-0

Typeset in 10.5pt Baskerville Win95BT

Production Manager: Chris Cowlin

Cover Design: Siobhan Smith

Printed and bound in Great Britain

The author, Billy Roberts has his own website: **www.billyroberts.co.uk**

To my wife Dolly, for her love and support, and also to Pesi, the elderly lady (pussycat) of the house. Their cuddles helped me with the writing immensely.

I would also like to thank my friend, Ciaran O'Keeffe for taking the time to write the foreword.

FOREWORD

Aura is a term now permanently ingrained in the English speaking vocabulary. The various definitions range from the more spiritually focused concerning "energy emanations" and "etheric substances" to the more medical such as "seizure or migraine warnings." What is obvious is that whilst New Age practices promote its importance in healing and in assessing the emotional or spiritual state of a person, science has a very different view. There are possible natural explanations that are to do with retinal fatigue and the aforementioned epileptic seizures or onset of migraines and even fraud. In addition, a perfectly logical account exists for Kirlian photography. What Billy does in the following words is to give you the spiritual side to auras. He combines his personal experiences with 'how to' instructions and the essence of auras in such seemingly disparate supernatural phenomena as OBEs and astrology. In addition, there is frequent mention of historical precursors to auras (e.g. Native American Indian, religious saints etc). It is due to this historical context and the personal insight that I thought it appropriate to write a foreword. For, even though I favour the more skeptical explanations for auras and aura readings it is imperative that the reader is given ample knowledge to be able to question. Knowing that the fundamental message here is that it is all based on Billy's personal experiences and that you, too, can try it for yourself, means that it is a book of research. Although the research method would not stand up to rigorous scrutiny by the scientific community, before we dismiss the aura out of hand it is worthwhile mentioning recent cognitive neuropsychological research into the link between synaesthesia and auras. Synaesthesia is a condition in which stimulation of one sense produces a response in one or more of the other senses (e.g. synaesthetics may experiences smells with sounds). One condition is known as 'emotion color synaesthesia'. As you take the following journey of factual and experiential discovery constantly ask the question, does science hold the answer or are auras truly a spiritual phenomena?

Ciarán O'Keeffe

Dr. Ciarán O'Keeffe
TV Parapsychologist (Most Haunted)

CONTENTS

	Introdcution	1
1.	The Aura throughout History	5
2.	What is the Aura and How is it Perceived?	8
3.	Seeing the Aura for Yourself	14
4.	The Aura and the Universe	22
5.	The Aura and Positive Thinking	25
6.	Science Looks at Psychic Skills	30
7.	Psychic Self-Defence and the Aura	35
8.	Developing Psychic Skills	41
9.	How to Cultivate the Senses	44
10.	Dowsing the Aura	48
11.	The Aura and Healing	52
12.	Chakras - The Whirlpools Within	55
13.	The Aura and Colour	62
14.	Checking out your Balance	69
15.	Creating the right Atmosphere	73
16.	Focusing the Powers of the Mind	78
17.	Encouraging the Image-Making Faculty	87
18.	Looking Forward Through Time	96
19.	Tuning the Aura and your Key of Life	104
20.	Chanting your way to a More Fulfiled Life	109
21.	Meditation - The key to Self-Mastery	114
22.	Psychic (Pranic) Healing	120
23.	Magnetic Healing for the Aura	126
24.	How Crystals affect the Aura	130
25.	The Science of the out-of-body Experience	137
26.	Colour Healing and the Aura	145
27.	The Aura of Enviroment	151
28.	Astrological Influences on the Aura	155

INTRODUCTION

Having been psychic since I was a child, I have always been aware of the aura in one way or another. Although I didn't know then that what I was seeing was actually called the 'aura', I was aware that the vaporous mist I saw around things and people somehow gave me a much deeper insight into the life around me. When I now look back I realise that what I saw emanating from flowers, plants and trees showed perfect balance and rarely changed, except when the seasons gradually moved from one to another; whereas, what I could see around people constantly changed in appearance, from one moment to the next, and that change somehow reflected their moods and the way they felt generally. As a consequence, this affected the way I felt about those whose energies I could see.

It was only in my mid-teens that I really began to make a detailed analysis of the aura and seriously tried to interpret and understand its true meaning. I had always been fascinated by the kaleidoscopic appearance of the aura and the way it could metamorphose, seemingly of its own accord. I wanted desperately to know what caused this spontaneous transformation, and more importantly why we even have an aura at all.

Even in psychic parlance, the aura is frequently misunderstood. Although most people say, "This room has an aura of peace" or "He has an aura of mystery about him", it did not take me very long to conclude that the aura was far more than a descriptive term, and that it is a scientific fact - a metaphysical phenomenon. I really only became confused about the aura when I began working as a medium on the spiritualist circuit. Listening to mediums talking about the colours they could see around people, and what they thought those colours meant, not only confused me but also made me wonder if we were actually talking about the same phenomenon. I began reading as much as I could on the subject of the aura and even explored the concept of the aura as portrayed in various ancient cultures. The more I explored, the more confused I became. At that point I concluded that I had to look more closely at what I already knew about this incredible phenomenon. Left to my own devices, I began making a detailed analysis of my own experiences. Although I thought I knew quite a lot about the aura, as it turned out I knew only a minute portion of what there actually was to know. During the course of my research I discovered that this was the case with so many mediums working on the spiritualist circuit today. Unfortunately, the majority of mediums who are able to 'see' a small part of the aura mistakenly believe that this is all there is to see of this incredible phenomenon that plays such an important part in the manifestation of consciousness. In fact, what the majority of mediums are seeing is only a minute part of an even greater whole.

Although the aura itself is not a 'sixth sense', it does exist as a sort of radar screen and filter, somehow integrating with the faculties and consciousness. But what is the aura, and what is its purpose? This is the question that has baffled religious academics, scientists and esoteric teachers for thousands of years. Today, though, there is a more scientific approach to unravelling the mystery of the aura, and in more recent years ways to capture its photographic image have been developed. Before this amazing advance, the existence of the aura remained a mystery and was left to the writer's imagination. The real breakthrough came when Semyon and Valentina Kirlian, a husband and wife team from Krasnodar near the Black Sea, developed a crude apparatus to photograph the aura emanating from the hands. The Kirlians used the developed image produced by their crude device as a diagnostic tool. By making a detailed analysis of the monochrome image of the energy radiating from the hands, the couple believed that information could be gleaned about the entire anatomical structure. Some time later, 'screens' were developed containing a special dye, which enabled the user, when looking through them, to 'see' the auric field. These screens were developed by Dr Walter Kilner, a radiologist at St Thomas's Hospital, London. Dr Kilner's extensive studies of the human aura led him to write a book about it entitled *The Human Atmosphere*, later retitled *The Aura*. This book was, in fact, an inspiration to others working in the same field, and gave rise to further research on the aura. Kilner was reputed to be the first man to observe the aura scientifically and, as a result of his research, many diseases can now be diagnosed and thus treated through the body's subtle energies. Today, however, modern technology has advanced so far that the entire aura may now be photographed in colour, complete with a computerised printed interpretation.

Although a photograph of the aura may be used more practically as a diagnostic tool, spiritual data about the person may also be gleaned. In fact, the aura may be regarded as a personal computer, in which all the data relating to the individual's life are stored. Anyone with auric vision may access a vast reservoir of spiritual, emotional and physical information, enabling the seer to gain greater control of his or her life. It must be said, though, that once one is able to 'see' the aura, the actual art of being able to use that skill must be cultivated before the quality of one's life can be improved. Perceiving a person's aura is not enough; a detailed analysis must be made of what is seen, and the conclusions then recorded.

In more recent years, scientific studies have been conducted in various countries on the phenomenon of bioluminescence - the generation and transmission of light by living organisms. The bioluminescent properties of the physical body are believed, by some scientists, to be contributory factors to the phenomenon of the aura, an outward manifestation of an inwardly created light. I have made a detailed analysis of the various phenomena of the aura and have explored its possibilities and broader implications. After studying the aura and related phenomena for over 25 years, I came to the conclusion that there was a need for a handbook that contained easy-to-follow methods explaining how to expand and use the aura. It was my intention to create a simple programme consisting of meditation techniques and other practical methods suitable for the layman as well as the working psychic. I have used many of the following techniques in my workshops all over the world, and my development programme has helped many aspiring psychics to develop and refine their skills.

3

In the following study of the aura I have also included many other paranormal manifestations resulting from this fascinating phenomenon, and also explain exactly how awareness of the aura can help you to gain greater control of your life.

Whether you are an aspiring psychic or medium, or just someone who is seeking to attain success and happiness, the magic of the aura will help you - so, read on ...

CHAPTER ONE
THE AURA
THROUGHOUT HISTORY

There is much historical evidence for the existence of the aura. For instance, the halo traditionally seen around the heads of saints in medieval paintings was in actual fact a symbolisation of that part of the aura that represented the divine nature of the individual. The very fact that the artists painted the halo at all shows that they must have been aware of the aura's existence, even though the subtle glow of golden light that they painted around the head is a mere part of what actually is to be seen in the aura as a whole. For when the aura is seen in its entirety it obscures the whole body with colour and movement, and extends outwards from it into the surrounding space.

The multicoloured headdress of the Native American chief was in fact also worn to symbolise the aura. The different coloured feathers represented his exalted position in the tribe; the more coloured feathers he wore, the higher his spiritual status. However, the coloured feathers were not simply inherited with the position of chief. On the contrary, the warrior had to prove that he was morally and spiritually worthy to receive them. Once done, the headdress was worn with great pride.

The tonsure (shaven head) of the monk was not just some kind of aberration that caught on in monastic quarters; it was intended to expose that part of the mind to divine consciousness, effectively laying bare the aura around the head to God and cosmic influences. The hair was thought to be unclean, thus inhibiting the flow of spiritual force, and it is significant that this procedure also laid bare the crown chakra (see Chapter 12 for a detailed discussion of the chakra system).

Some Eastern cultures took this ideology to the extreme by

carrying out invasive surgery to expose the brow centre to cosmic forces. A frontal lobotomy was performed by inserting a fine wooden stake between the brows. This horrific procedure was carried out on some monks and their devotees, primarily to encourage a heightened state of consciousness. Although seven out of ten of those subjected to this procedure eventually died, the ones that survived did achieve some sort of transcendental awareness and were revered with some degree of respect. Although this procedure is most certainly not recommended, the very fact that it was practised at all does prove that transcendental states of awareness have always been an integral part of some religious cultures.

There are also many references to the aura in the Bible, the most popular one being Joseph's coat of many colours. Also, when Moses descended from Mount Sinai with the Ten Commandments, it is said that his face shone so his people were unable to look at him. Ezekiel saw the aura as a rainbow, and in the book of Revelation the aura appeared like white wool to Saint John.

Medieval mystics said that man emitted light just like stars in the heavens. In fact, from time immemorial man has made some sort of reference to a light radiating from the human form. The Aztecs spoke about flames of light streaming from the heads of their spiritual leaders, and ancient murals have depicted holy men with an incredible atmosphere about them. There is too much historical evidence for us to dismiss the existence of the aura, and today's available scientific apparatus substantiates the claims made by ancient writers and mystics that the aura does exist.

For centuries there have been references made to certain old buildings or even geographical locations having an aura about them, and although the word aura is more than a descriptive term, we do tend to use it to describe the feeling we get from places as well as people. For example, 'This house has an aura of warmth', or 'She has an aura of peace about her'. Most people use the word 'aura' without really understanding its true metaphysical implications, even though most do have a fundamental grasp of its meaning.

The greater the radiance surrounding a person, the more apparent their goodness and spirituality. A clear and bright auric bioluminescence is an indication that the individual is very well balanced on all levels, and that their health is good and their intentions quite honourable. It is quite easy to see at this point just what advantages there are in being able actually to 'see' the aura, and that just being able to 'feel' the aura would allow you to access a great deal of personal data about an individual. However, sometimes these skills present some disadvantages, as the seer may 'see' something he or she would sooner not have seen.

CHAPTER TWO
WHAT IS THE AURA AND
HOW IS IT PERCEIVED?

The aura is best described as a vaporous mass of electromagnetic particles surrounding both animate and inanimate matter. It is, in fact, an energy field of an extremely subtle nature. However, the aura that emanates from the human form differs in more ways than one from that which emanates from an inanimate object, for the human aura represents the degree (level) of life and consciousness present. Although the presence of consciousness and life in both animate and inanimate matter is measured in degrees, the aura emanating from animate matter is completely different in both appearance and movement to that which emanates from inanimate matter, even though life is still present in the inanimate state, albeit at a much lower level. In fact, in comparison to the aura of an inanimate object, the human energy field is a veritable kaleidoscope of colours, and is full of movement as it radiates outwards from the body. In the human aura the degree or level of vitality present in the body is exhibited in the consistency of radiation lines and in the combinations and frequency of colours, their shades and their clarity.

The human aura is in fact more luminous than the inanimate aura and changes with every passing thought, feeling and emotion. Therefore, the one who is able to perceive the human aura in its totality is able to gain access to an abundance of personal information about the individual from whom it emanates.

Although the aura is a subtle, vaporous mass of electromagnetic particles surrounding every living thing, it may, to some extent, be perceived by the peripheral sight of the physical eyes. In other words, the aura is often seen out of the corner of the eye even though the seer may not realise exactly what it is he or she is seeing. Although it is primarily a subtle energy, the majority of people are capable of perceiving the aura's physical manifestation without any effort at all. In fact, this is the primary reason why there is so much confusion within the mediumistic profession regarding the aura and the meaning of its colours. In fact, it seems to be quite fashionable amongst psychics and mediums to talk about the aura as though seeing it was quite commonplace and a phenomenon to which all psychics are privy. This is a misconception. Even though the aura has psychic and spiritual connotations, and is a phenomenon usually associated with the psychic abilities of mediums etc., its existence is now a scientific fact, and although there are conflicting ideas as to what exactly the aura is, its existence can most certainly be scientifically proved. It must be said, however, that although the majority of psychics are able to sense the aura, only a small percentage of them are actually able to 'see' it.

The physical aura is the most apparent, but it is only a small part of a much greater whole. The aura emanating from the physical body is usually the easiest to perceive and extends no more than five to six inches from the body into the surrounding space. Its colour is usually white or very pale blue and has a luminous appearance, making it quite visible even in the dark. The aura in its entirety is quite extensive, and one of the most common misconceptions is that the aura's extent reflects the person's spirituality. This is a fallacy and an extremely unhealthy one at that. The spiritual status of the person is reflected in the intensity, shades and degrees of the colours and not in the extent or size of the aura. Although the individual colours must be considered when making a detailed analysis of the aura (for whatever reason), the overall appearance and combinations of the colour arrangements have to be included in the final analysis.

As far back as I can recall, I have been able to look directly at a person's aura and 'see' an extremely intense vaporous light. As a child I had to look at it for some time before colour was gradually introduced. However, even when there was only a grey-blue vapour around a person, I sensed quite a lot more than those colours told me. Even people who cannot see the aura at all often sense it without realising it. In fact, it is the auras (aurae) of things and people that cause you to have a sense of 'something' in the surrounding atmosphere. It is through the aura that feelings are sensed about people you meet for the first time. I am quite sure that most of us have had the experience of walking into an old (or sometimes new) building only to be overwhelmed with feelings of warmth or coldness. A building too has an aura and it is this that gives it character and personality. Human magnetism impregnates the solid structure of a building, and the longer a person lives in a particular house, the more his or her personality interacts with the subtle nature of that house. Solid structure somehow encapsulates energy, and the energy discharged from the human and animal mind is able to infiltrate matter and, as a result, be perpetuated. It is this interaction of energy that frequently leads mediums and psychics mistakenly to believe that they are communicating with discarnate spirits.

UNIVERSAL ENERGY
Prana is the Sanskrit word that denotes all energy in the universe, and a little knowledge of Prana is essential when endeavouring to cultivate a more vibrant and intense aura. In the ancient traditions of yoga, Prana is believed to be the subtle agent through which the life of the body is sustained. By drawing in excessive amounts of Prana one is able to increase one's quality of life. When the levels of Prana in the body are reduced, a corresponding effect on the overall vitality is experienced. Prana is believed to be the principle responsible for the integration of the cells into a whole. In other words, Prana 'binds' all things together and is essential for the maintenance of health. Whilst the air we breathe is a primary source of Prana, it is not the air itself. Even though Prana is found running through all forms of matter, it is not matter. Water is an extremely vibrant source of Prana but it is not Prana. When Prana is completely absent in the physical body death occurs. As Prana is an integral part of the cultivation of the aura it will be referred to all through this book.

THE AURA OF A DEAD PERSON

When a person has just died, his or her aura can be seen moving quickly from the feet to the head in a spiralling motion. It is discharged through the top of the head, at which point it dissipates into a display of innumerable pinpoints of sparkling light, rather like an effervescent tablet dropped into a glass of water. Once all the energies have been discharged from the body, the spiralling movement gradually loses its momentum, taking on an opaque appearance of a pale grey colour. At the conclusion of this phenomenon the aura appears still and almost lifeless. The aura at this point represents the amount of Prana still present in the body, performing its function of integrating the cells into a whole unit. When the body has decayed and subsequently disintegrated, the individual cells that comprise the physical body begin to run amok. They take with them sufficient Prana to enable them to form new combinations. And so we can see that even with the death of the physical body there is still life. The human aura is an incredibly powerful force, and represents man on innumerable levels.

THE SUBTLE ANATOMY

Man is a far more complex being than is generally imagined. He possesses a subtle anatomy as well as a physical one, and this is stabilised by strategically situated vortexes called 'chakras', whose primary function is to control the inflowing universal energy. Chakras are like transformers, modifying, dividing and distributing the inflowing energy to the organs of the physical body and maintaining balance between the physical and the subtle anatomies. Although there are hundreds of minor chakras throughout the subtle anatomy, there are, in fact, seven major chakras that are considered primary. These are situated across the surface of the etheric tract in the spinal column, and their vibratory rate increases as they ascend the spine. The seven major chakras are connected to the endocrine glands and nerve plexuses through an extensive system of channels, the esoteric word for which is 'nadis'. The word Nadi means nerve only at a more subtle level. Nadis criss-cross the subtle anatomy, connecting the chakras in a serpentine fashion, from the lowest at the base of the spine to the highest on the crown of the head. Chakras are responsible for the evolution of consciousness, and their development encourages the cultivation of psychic skills. The word 'chakra' literally means 'wheel' or 'circle' in Sanskrit, and as the development of the faculties takes place the vibratory motion of each individual chakra is greatly increased as a direct consequence.

Each of the major chakras has a different polarity, and the chakra system of a man has an opposite vibratory motion to that of a woman. Once each individual chakra has been correctly polarised through their development, the person's aura reflects this with an increase in its sharpness, intensity and vitality. This means then that a psychic person's aura is much more colourful, particularly when he or she is actually using their psychic skills.

APPARITIONS AND THE AURA

So-called 'apparitions' are frequently no more than photographic images in the psycho-etheric atmosphere; a sort of replay of events that have long since gone. Strong emotions released into the atmosphere have a tendency to impregnate the physical structures around them with vivid impressions of those from whose minds they originated in the first place. Very often what is seen in an apparition, or so-called 'ghost', is an exact image of the person as he or she was at the point of death. This image is perpetuated by the energy that was released through the person's aura when he or she was alive, thus creating the apparition. As these sorts of ghostly images are no more than photographic replays in the atmosphere, they have no intelligence or awareness of their surroundings. Images such as these often persist for hundreds of years and are perpetuated by certain geological structures which energise and sustain them. Old stone and sandstone structures built close to water, for instance, are nearly always epicentres of paranormal activity. Water creates its own energy and this has an extremely powerful interactive effect on the geological components of the building itself, causing a variety of paranormal phenomena. However, not all ghostly phenomena are the products of atmos-pherically impregnated energy.

There are exceptions, for example when discarnate spirits simply refuse to move on, choosing instead to continue living in the environment with which they have always been familiar. This is a completely different phenomenon and, unlike the photographic images, these apparitions do have a degree of intelligence and an awareness of their environment. In most cases, however, they are only aware of the environment as they knew it and not as it is in the present.

The photographic image phenomenon does not have an obvious aura, whereas a discarnate apparition is always surrounded by an intense luminous light. In fact, this is what differentiates the two phenomena and enables a real ghost to be distinguished from a lifeless impression in the psychic space.

The aura is the common denominator and it is through this that one is able to access an incredible paranormal reservoir of data. In fact, the aura is a subtle blueprint of another dimension. Once the aura is fully understood and one is able to decipher it, a greater and more profound comprehension of both the physical and invisible worlds is developed as a consequence. Through a deeper understanding of the aura that surrounds you, it is possible to cultivate your intuition to such an extent that you will be able to 'read' things and other people. Learning to use your own aura will enable you to access the 'memory' of all things around you, and as a result will encourage greater control of your life.

CHAPTER THREE
SEEING THE AURA
FOR YOURSELF

I am quite certain that most of us have had the experience of being totally engrossed in conversation, completely unaware that time has passed by, only to find that our eyes have gone completely out of focus, mainly because we have been concentrating intently. The person to whom we are speaking also goes out of focus, and although at the time we don't really notice it a shadow or band of light becomes apparent around the other person's head. This is usually seen out of the peripheral vision, and when it is looked at directly it disappears completely. In fact, this is the nature of the untrained eye, and the whole process of 'seeing' the aura is one of training. When we are engrossed in conversation, the retina of the eye becomes tired and the visual response mechanism is thrown into states of confusion and fatigue. The image-making faculty of the mind then becomes active, enabling the impressions of the aura to be processed quickly by the brain. As with anything, though, practice does make perfect, and before you can successfully achieve the development of auric vision you must make a systematic analysis of your experiences.

The majority of those analysing the aura do so through their own experiences with it. However, as each person's experience with the aura is subjective it is difficult to say exactly what it is he or she is actually seeing. Anyone can describe a beautiful autumnal sunset, but it is the descriptive skill of the one who has a keen eye for detail that is able to provide the most effective and more graphic description. When training to 'see' the aura, focus on the detail and, instead of looking at the obvious, pay careful attention to what is not so apparent. There are aspects to the aura that only become apparent when you stare intently at it. This is why scrying is used as a tool to cultivate the skill of 'seeing' the aura. Making

14

the eyes go out of focus activates the visual response mechanism and encourages them to actually 'see' the aura more clearly.

THE FIRST STEP TO SEEING THE AURA
Exercise One
For this exercise you will need to enlist the help of a friend (at least someone who understands what you are endeavouring to achieve).
* Make sure that the lighting in the room in which you are working is fairly subdued.
* Stand the person against a light background, and engage yourselves in conversation. Do not make any attempt whatsoever to 'see' anything.
* Focus your attention on your partner's chin or neck area, and use your peripheral vision to see their aura.
* At first you will not see anything at all, but when your eyes become tired and slightly out of focus, a shadow or band of light will become apparent around his or her head. This will appear to glow and will be almost translucent. It is important not to look at this and just keep staring at your partner.
* If you persist with the exercise and continue to gaze, you will eventually 'see' the beginning stages of the aura. Once you know exactly what it is you are looking for, your eyes should become more accustomed to it and even more of the aura should eventually become apparent.

Exercise Two
Here is another simple experiment to help you 'see' what the aura looks like:
* Remove the dark pips from an apple. (Make sure they are dark and not white pips.)
* Place two pips on a white piece of paper.
* Stare at the pips for a few moments, preferably with the lighting subdued.
* Slightly relax your gaze but do not allow yourself to be distracted even for a moment.
* Within a few seconds you will begin to see a faint pale blue or white glow around each of the pips. The glow will appear to

radiate outwards and may move around the pips in a clockwise motion.

* Remove the pips from the paper and place them in an envelope for 24 hours.
* The following day retrieve the pips from the envelope and place them once again on a white piece of paper, and now see how the radiations of energy have diminished.
* The pips now represent a sick or dying person, whose aura is depleted.
* For the final part of the experiment, remove some more pips from a fresh apple and then place these on the paper approximately half an inch away from the old pips.
* Now, see how the energy radiating from the new pips extends towards the old pips, almost in an asserted effort to revitalise them.

This is an example of energy transference, a natural process that all healthy people experience when in the presence of someone who is unwell.

The energy radiating from the apple pips represents the health aura seen around people. When the aura is bright and sharp, the person is usually in good health; when it is dull and fairly sluggish, the person is in poor health.

Examples of this phenomenon will be given later on in the book.

SEEING YOUR OWN AURA
Exercise One
For this experiment you will need to stand in front of a long mirror in a dark room:

* First of all, spend a few minutes standing in front of the mirror, and stare at your nose without blinking.
* When everything goes out of focus, clear your eyes by looking away from the mirror.
* Return your gaze to your reflection, and stare at your nose once again.
* However, this time when everything begins to go out of focus slowly move your gaze downwards from your nose to your chest.
* Resist the temptation to look away from the mirror.

* Allow your gaze to follow a straight line as far as you can down your body, and then move it upwards again in a straight line back to your nose.
* Now, allow your gaze to rest on your nose and, using your peripheral vision, notice the luminous glow around your body.
* Do not move your eyes to look directly at it, but maintain the gaze and watch the glow through your peripheral vision.
* By now the luminous glow should appear quite bright and clear.
* When you feel quite confident, gradually move your eyes to look directly at the glow.
* Once you have mastered the exercise and can look directly at your aura, stare at it and, using the same process as before, allow your peripheral sight to see even more of your aura.
* Do not practise for more than twenty minutes at a time, as any longer will merely cause eye strain and defeat the whole object of the exercise.

Exercise Two
Once again, stand in front of a mirror in a darkened room:
* Shake your hands vigorously for about a minute, or until you can feel them tingle.
* Press the palms of your hands together in front of you, and then slowly pull them apart. As you do so, stare intently between them without actually looking directly at them.
* Repeat the process over and over again until you can see a luminous band of light around your hands. This will probably disappear if you look directly at it.
* Repeat the exercise, only this time try looking at the reflection of your hands in the mirror. The luminous glow from your hands should be reflected and cause a glow in the room.

Again, once the technique has been mastered, you should have a fairly good idea exactly what the aura looks like. You may even like to try the same experiment with objects such as a chair, a table or even a picture on the wall. Remember, even inanimate objects have an aura, albeit it at a much lower level than people and animals.

Once you have familiarised yourself with the aura around your hands, you should be able to see the same glow around the heads and even the whole bodies of a few people.

AURIC FRAGMENTATIONS

Occasionally a person's aura throws off sparks of energy, often called 'fragmentations'. These may appear to you as pinpoints of light around the person's head. They are often dismissed as being no more than tricks of the light or the product of tired eyes, or even static electricity. These are probably the reasons why the majority of people take no notice of them and disregard the phenomenon completely. These sparkling pinpoints of light often occur when the person is full of energy. In fact, standing close to someone like this is very therapeutic, particularly when one is feeling a little run down or under the weather.

THE AURA OF A VISUALLY HANDICAPPED PERSON

In my studies of the aura I have always found it to be more sensitive at the back of a person, and in fact proportionately more extensive than at the front. However, this does not seem to be the case with a visually handicapped person, where the aura appears to extend equally all around the body. The absence of sight causes the aura at the front to be more developed than is the case with a sighted person. The extra development takes place in order to compensate for the absence of sight, and usually allows the sensitivity and awareness of the visually handicapped person to be heightened. In other words, the aura is our 'antennae' and, surrounding us completely, is constantly sensing the environment around us for signs of danger. When a detailed analysis is made of the aura one can see that it is not a separate entity independent of our body, but is in fact an integral part of our subtle nature, and is merely an extension of our spiritual self or consciousness.

THE SEVEN BODIES

We are seven-fold beings, even whilst we live in a physical world. Although the physical body is the most apparent of all our bodies, we do possess other more subtle vehicles, each one composed of a much finer material than the one below it. Each of these bodies relates to a different plane of the universe and is thus responsible for the manifestation of consciousness on each of those planes. In fact, each of our subtle bodies radiates energy, and it is the combination of all these radiations that constitutes the aura, the electromagnetic field of energy that surrounds all living things. To all intents and purposes, the physical body itself is an incredible powerhouse of energy and, although it is the most apparent of all our bodies, it should not in any way be underestimated. The individual cells that comprise the physical body constantly vibrate, and it is the energy created from this vibratory motion that actually produces the physical aura. The same applies to all the other bodies, only at a more subtle level.

THE AURA'S MAGIC

The human organism is an electromagnetic unit of tremendous power, appropriating, assimilating and releasing energy. It is contained within its own field of light and colour, radiating both towards and away from its inner centre. This magnetic field, the aura, interpenetrates the physical body and also reaches out to integrate with other energies. Even though the majority of people do not even know that the aura exists, they are still able to sense the surrounding environment through it.

Whether you can actually 'see' the aura or not, everyone can feel it and is, in more ways than one, influenced by it to some greater or lesser degree. Here are some examples to illustrate the point.

Example One

You may be taking a leisurely walk down a country lane, enjoying the beautiful sunshine and mentally drinking in the peace and tranquillity of the day, completely oblivious to anything other than the sunshine and the birds singing along your way. You eventually reach the shelter of trees on either side of the road, and at a certain point you suddenly become aware of a resistance in your muscular movements. Something has caused an alteration in the rhythm of your step, making you aware of someone approaching. This may be a friend hurrying to catch your attention, or simply someone following the same route as you. Because you were engrossed in the peacefulness of your walk your other senses failed to make you aware that you were not alone. However, the electromagnetic waves from the other person's aura interfered with the electromagnetic atmosphere from your own body. Your own personal radar system was scanning the area and reported back to you that you were not alone, and through your subconsciousness your muscle response was changed.

Example Two
You may be sitting in a theatre audience of hundreds of people, listening to the background music and waiting for the show to begin. Suddenly, something makes you feel uncomfortable and you turn around to look in a certain direction only to see someone glaring at you from behind. You could not have known that the person was looking at you, but something made you turn around. In fact, his or her electromagnetic radiation interfered with yours and through your subconsciousness you involuntarily moved your eyes in that direction. Although this phenomenon is frequently referred to as 'instinct', it is caused by an interference of psycho-magnetic radiation, or an interruption of your auric waves through your subconsciousness.

When a crowd of people come together, as is the case with a theatre audience, for example, each person's aura closes up into an egg-like shell, ensuring their safety and protection from their external surroundings. Once each person relaxes, the collective aurae exhibit a beautiful kaleidoscopic display of innumerable iridescent colours, filling the atmosphere with energy and vitality. In fact, the aurae of an audience enjoying the melodic sounds of a symphonic orchestra are something to behold, and appear like a swirling multicoloured mist filling the entire theatre.

Example Three
How often have you suddenly been overwhelmed with a feeling that a family member or even a friend is in trouble and is going to phone you, and so you are not surprised when they do? As I have previously stated, your aura is your personal psycho-magnetic

radar system, and is constantly scanning the surrounding space, just like a military radar scanning the airways for enemy missiles.

Example Four
This example is given more to prove the existence of an electro-magnetic atmosphere surrounding you than it is to show what it does for you:

Tune a transistor radio into any station on the VHF frequency, and then fold down the aerial so that the programme is lost and all that you can hear is white noise. Then place your right hand over the folded aerial and extend your left arm in front of you, moving it around until the station is located clearly once again.

This simple experiment proves that your aura is a conductor of electromagnetic energy of immense power and possesses the capacity to attract waves of energy from other sources. Your aura replaced the radio's aerial sufficiently for a clear reception to be maintained. Thus, if the electromagnetic atmosphere surrounding you has the capacity to receive such waves of energy, it must also have the capacity to transmit the same.

Once you are able to perceive the aura in this way, the whole of nature will take on a completely different appearance and meaning. Of course, whether you can 'see' the aura or not is not that important. The aura is your personal radar system and through it you are able to 'home in', so to speak, to the energies of your surrounding environment. This means you have a natural ability to access the personal database of other people, and the means of mentally acquiring information stored in the memory of things and even places. The more you exercise your aura, the stronger and more vibrant it becomes.

The aura is truly a magical phenomenon and the primary cause of countless human phenomena, and through its cultivation and development innumerable psychic skills may be produced.

CHAPTER FOUR
THE AURA AND
THE UNIVERSE

Sceptics would no doubt dismiss the notion that their personal energies extend beyond the confines of their own physical body to thus interact with the energies of the universe. To understand this concept more fully it is important to have a deeper comprehension of the vibratory structure of the aura in relation to the universe itself.

We live, to all intents and purposes, in a multidimensional universe in which there are worlds within worlds, each rising in a gradually ascending vibratory scale, from those that touch and blend with the highest planes of the physical world, to those that gradually merge with the lowest planes of the astral world. It is an axiom of physics that no two bodies of matter can occupy the same space at the same time; but millions upon millions of vibrations can and do exist in the one space without interfering with one another. The human form is far more than simply a collection of cells with a life expectancy of three score years and ten and destined for complete annihilation through some chemical and physiological change called 'death'. Even scientists are now looking at the possibility that death may not be the end, and that we are capable of much, much more!

The energy created by the overall components of the physical body radiates outwards into the surrounding space, infusing the energies of the universe and ultimately interacting with them. When a baby is born into this world there is usually a state of total equilibrium between mind, body and soul, and this is only interrupted when the child is old enough to be programmed by its parents, circumstances and life itself. It is this interruption that causes disorientation within the aura, facilitating a state of chaos and disharmony and throwing the aura into disarray and thus out of sync with the universe. Of course, if the child has wise parents who themselves have a deeper spiritual understanding, the growing infant is more in control by adult life and may ultimately be more positive and successful as a consequence.

Once the aura lapses into a state of chaos, a corresponding effect is produced on the individual's life. A disorientated aura sends out negative signals into the universe, and as a consequence is then drawn towards people and situations sympathetically in tune.

Everything in the universe is constantly vibrating, and within that vibration can be found a certain rhythm. In fact, rhythm pervades the entire universe, producing perfect sequence and order. When we cease to be synchronised with this universal rhythm things go drastically wrong in our lives. This disharmony becomes apparent as either disease or as an insurmountable problem. We all know that feeling only too well: one problem follows another, and it's always difficult to get straight, almost as though we have been cursed. The mind is the common denominator when endeavouring to restore the aura's equilibrium. Smoothing out the rough edges of the aura and repairing fragmentations may be achieved by using a psychological process of rhythmic breathing. Rhythmic breathing not only restores stability to the aura but also helps to repair fragmentations and encourage vitality.

RHYTHMIC BREATHING EXERCISE

* Sit comfortably on a straight-backed chair, with your shoulders thrown slightly backwards, and your chest and head as nearly in a straight line as possible.
* Ascertain your normal heartbeat by placing your fingers on your pulse, counting mentally with each heartbeat.
[The rhythmic time is based on a unit of each heartbeat, and the units of inhalation and exhalation should always be the same, whilst the units of retention and between breaths should be one-half the number of inhalation and exhalation.]
* Once you have established the rhythm of your heart fully in your mind, with your eyes closed breathe in to the count of six heartbeats, hold it for the count of three, exhale to the count of six

23

and then hold it again for the count of three.

* Repeat this breathing pattern for approximately 8 to 10 minutes. Do not strain your breathing or make it a labour as this merely defeats the whole object of the exercise, which is to promote calmness and equilibrium.

* Should you find it difficult to breathe in and out to the count of six, you can begin initially to the count of four, reducing the retentions proportionately to the count of two in order to maintain a steady rhythm.

* Once you have become accustomed to this technique of rhythmic breathing and feel quite comfortable with it, you can increase the number of inhalations and exhalations.

To achieve maximum results this exercise should be practised on rising in the morning and again before retiring at night. Rhythmic breathing will encourage quietness and serenity, and may therefore be used before any meditation period as a means of preparing the mind.

Although rhythmic breathing affects all people differently, if practised daily positive results should be achieved within three to four months. The first signs should be seen in one's sleep pattern, which should be more restful and consistent. One should also feel more alert with a gradual memory improvement.

CHAPTER FIVE
THE AURA AND POSITIVE
THINKING

The aura is undoubtedly the key to a more fulfilled and successful life. Negative thinking very often begins in the aura before infiltrating the mind. If allowed to persist, the forces that drive you into that negative state will eventually manifest externally as conditions and circumstances. A little understanding of the aura can help free you from the shackles of negative thinking and help you to build a stronger and more positive and vibrant character. Such a psychological transformation eventually produces its corresponding effect on your whole life. A deeper realisation of the aura can also precipitate the natural healing properties of the mind and thus aid the development of a more healthy body. First of all, though, you need to acknowledge the fact that the aura does exist. Once you have accepted that you do have an energy field surrounding you, and that it is multicoloured and extremely vibrant, you can begin to take control of your own destiny.

When someone is ecstatically happy, they 'shine', and being in their presence is extremely invigorating and is like a tonic to us. Conversely, spending too long in the company of someone who is depressed and unhappy also produces a similar effect on us, making us feel despondent and quite low. Although depression can descend on us at any time, it may well be that the dark cloud around you has been produced as a consequence of the environment in which you live. Districts, towns and even nations have subtle atmospheres, created by all those who live there or have done so throughout the years. A happy, contented family living in an oppressive, disharmonious environment will soon become like the place in which they live, just as a happy and peaceful location will eventually transform misery into happiness.

When you are feeling under the weather, or perhaps a little depressed, your auric emanations become sluggish and dull. This condition is transmitted to all those with whom you come into contact. Depression tends to affect those around you, and when allowed to persist it eventually blends with the subtle nature of your environment. It then becomes an integral part of the psychic nature of the place in which you live and helps to create the very fabric of the atmosphere around you. In fact, each person's aura absorbs energy particles from the environment in which he or she lives. These particles are the fragmented emotions discharged by human minds, and which float around the psychic atmosphere until they eventually infiltrate the energy fields of those of a similar nature. When one has become accustomed to thinking in a negative way, it is very difficult to break free from the habit. Negative thinking is habitual, and we know only too well that once it takes a firm hold it is extremely difficult to interrupt the cycle. All health conditions, whether physical or psychological, become apparent in the aura before manifesting in the body. Therefore, actually preventing infiltration into the body is purely a psychological process.

HOW TO CLEANSE YOUR AURA

This following process is purely psychological and therefore must be practised at least once a day, preferably at night before you retire.

* Place some lighted candles strategically around the bathroom, pour a teaspoon of sea salt into a warm bath and swirl it around with your hand until it dissolves.

* Relax in the bath with your eyes closed for at least half an hour, and try to imbibe the restful atmosphere and serenity of the soothing warm water.

* Breathe deeply and rhythmically, ensuring that the inhalations and exhalations are evenly spaced (see rhythmic breathing exercise on page 23).

* Allow yourself to be aware of the warmth and pressure of the water against your skin, and feel the energy being absorbed into your very being.

* If comfortable, lie in the bath as low as you can, with the back of your head touching the water. Remain in that position for a few moments and then lower your head briefly, allowing your face to be completely submerged into the water.
* Hold that position with your eyes closed for as long as you feel comfortable, and imagine the warm water gently cleansing away all the impurities from your body and mind.

Although the majority find therapeutic value in taking a warm bath, it is believed that adding sea salt to the bathwater actually has a cleansing effect on the outer layers of the body, thus affecting the subtle anatomy. In addition to the lighted candles mentioned above, it can also be a good idea to play some relaxing music, as both help to create a soothing ambience and thus magnify the psychological effect and encourage a more serene aura.

SENDING OUT THE RIGHT SIGNALS

When we are stressed, worried or even feeling insecure, the aura becomes a little fragmented and less vibrant. Those with whom we come into contact are able to sense this and are very often affected by it. As I have previously said, the aura registers all emotional, psychological and spiritual feelings and has a tendency to be contagious. We are continually sending out signals into the surrounding space, impregnating the atmosphere with our own personal data. Most of us know what it is like to be in the presence of someone who is serene and calm - they affect us in the same way. Anxious or aggressive people affect us long before we make contact with them. Many people are sensitive to the subtle atmosphere of an old house, and can feel its happy or miserable vibrations. We all have an inbuilt radar system that enables us to home in on subtle atmospheres.

Animals rely on this radar system more than humans, and through this incredible ability are able to monitor molecular changes in the atmosphere, guiding them and warning them about approaching dangers. Because science and technology have advanced so much, we humans have become lazy and no longer have to rely on instinct as much as our prehistoric forebears did. However, with the use of some simple exercises we can make the aura much more efficient, stronger and more responsive to external forces. The advantages of this are incredibly helpful in the day-to-day running of our lives, and will encourage a more positive and dynamic approach to everyday situations.

The aura responds extremely well to thought, and by using a technique I call 'Auric Sculpturing' it is possible to extend your aura and encourage it to be more consistent. This means you will be able to influence people and situations to your advantage and, as a direct result, achieve your goals and attain success.

Auric Sculpturing and Sacred Space Exercise
* Find a quiet corner and sit in a comfortable chair. It is always a good idea to burn some pleasant incense - any fragrance that is pleasing to the senses.
* Now begin to relax your body as completely as you possibly can.
* With your eyes closed, begin to breathe slowly and deeply, allowing your stomach to rise as you breathe in, and letting it fall as you breathe out.
* Breathe rhythmically until the rhythm is fully established in your mind, making sure that the inhalations and exhalations are evenly spaced. To achieve the maximum results it is vitally important that this rhythm is maintained throughout the relaxation period.
* Fix your favourite colour in your mind, and imagine this colour passing further into your body each time you breathe in. Then, when you exhale, breathe out the first colour that comes to mind, making sure it is different to the one you breathed in.
* Be aware of the space surrounding you, and endeavour to feel a part of that space.
* Imagine that you are merely occupying your body temporarily, and that you may, therefore, leave it at any time you desire, knowing that you must always return to it, at least for the moment.
* See the space surrounding you as sacred and holy ground, and an area in which no one, whether seen or unseen, can move.
* Allow the space surrounding you to become slowly flooded with intense white light, whilst occasionally reminding yourself of the favourite colour you have been breathing in.

* Make your surrounding space strong and impenetrable by creating a high wall of vivid blue light around its circumference. Infuse the high wall with more energy, making it even more vibrant and powerful.

* Remain in this meditative state for a few minutes, making quite sure that your mind does not drift even for a moment, as this would merely defeat the object of the exercise.

Being aware of the inflowing and outflowing colours, at the same time as seeing your sacred space flooded with intense white light and also the high wall of vivid blue energy, may in fact prove quite difficult at first. Practice really will improve your ability to master this exercise. Once you can practise it with ease you will have learnt the art of peripheral focusing - the ability to think of several things at once. Once you have achieved this focusing technique your personal auric energies will be more efficient, stronger and more dynamic.

Although not always practical, to achieve maximum results it is a good idea to practise this exercise at least once a day, twice if possible. As I have previously explained, the object of the exercise is to cultivate peripheral focusing, the first step to gaining greater control of your life.

Even if you do not feel comfortable with the exercise and find it difficult to master, it is important to integrate it into your daily programme. As well as anything else, a strong and more dynamic aura will make you more resistant to illness and minor infections, such as colds and influenza. A healthy aura makes a healthier and much happier person. And a healthy and happy person is a person who is more in control.

CHAPTER SIX
SCIENCE LOOKS AT
PSYCHIC SKILLS

Today there is a growing interest in the paranormal and the science of psychic development. Having been psychic since I was a child it is now very difficult for me to imagine what it would be like not to be psychic. Having said that, I still had to refine and learn how to control my psychic skills instead of allowing them to control me. From a very early age I needed desperately to know why I had psychic abilities and how exactly they worked. I read as much as I could on the subject and made a detailed analysis of everything I had learned. Why are a lot of children psychic, and what makes one person more psychic than another? These were just some of the questions I needed to answer.

During my study of the subject I discovered that over the last 50 years far more research had been done in Russia and America, and that in these countries the subject was taken far more seriously than in the UK.

In 1903, Professor Tutinsky of Moscow University carried out extensive research into the workings of the brains of psychics and mediums. Although Tutinsky took pains to avoid the term 'psychic', his findings led him to conclude that the pineal gland, the walnut-shaped gland deep within the brain, played an extremely significant role in the manifestation of paranormal experiences. In fact, Tutinsky discovered that the pineal gland was larger in the child than it was in the adult, and significantly more developed in the female than in the male. Professor Tutinsky concluded that this was the reason why children often have psychic experiences, and why women are more psychically sensitive than men. This is probably the reason why a high percentage of male mediums are in fact effeminate or even gay. In his paper on the subject, the respected professor wrote that the human brain was capable of developing extraordinary powers that were outside the parameters of traditional science, and so therefore could not be measured by traditional scientific means.

Further research into paranormal abilities concluded that, regardless of what spiritualists believe, psychic and mediumistic skills are far from normal, and that there is a noticeable abnormality in the brain of a mediumistically inclined individual. In fact, when one gets involved in a psychic development programme, with the sole intention of cultivating the faculties, significant changes certainly do occur in the brain and nerve plexuses. It was found that these changes also affect the hormonal system by infusing specific points in the body with energy. The effects produced by the process of psychic development on the person's aura are extremely significant, and it is quite common for some mood changes to be experienced. For this reason alone, should an individual have a history of emotional or psychological problems, then it would be advisable to avoid any programme primarily intended to cultivate psychic abilities.

From time immemorial the belief that attaining higher states of consciousness will encourage the cultivation of extraordinary powers has been embraced by many cultures. In fact, some Eastern traditions have always advocated the disciplines of yoga as an effective way of developing psychic powers, or 'siddhis' as they are known, and others have recommended the use of meditation to expand the consciousness. Although these methods have been used successfully for thousands of years, a small minority chose a much quicker route: the practice of imbibing hallucinogenic substances to produce transcendental states. The hallucinogens were derived from a variety of naturally occurring plants, from Amanita Muscaria, the magical mushroom used in Shamanic rituals, to Mescaline, extracted from the button-shaped nodules of the Mexican Peyote spineless cactus, frequently used by Aztec priests. Another was Psilocybin, a crystalline hallucinogen, also obtained from the so-called 'sacred mushroom' used by a mystical sect known as the 'Mushroom People', whose whole spiritual philosophy was based on the hallucinogenic properties of the mushroom. In fact, hallucinogens have been an integral part of many spiritual cultures, and some even referred to the hallucinogenic substances they used as the 'nectar of the gods'. Whilst there can be no doubt that the hallucinogens did produce altered states of consciousness, some individuals never came out of the transcendental experience and the psychological damage produced a psychosis, making the user believe that he was actually a divine being. As a consequence, hallucinogens were only used by spiritually qualified individuals who imbibed the mind-altering substance when they needed to call on the spirits of their ancestors.

Hallucinogens affected the aura and its bioluminescence, encouraging it to extend and appear more vibrant. Of course, this metamorphosis was transitory, and more hallucinogens were needed to repeat the experience. In fact, the aura sustains serious, often irreparable damage when mind-altering substances are frequently used, and the safest and most effective method for expanding the consciousness is and always has been through the disciplines of meditation and yoga.

The aura is even significantly affected by prescribed medication, and anything that a person has been taking for long periods of time eventually causes the aura to become broken and fragmented. Frequent courses of antibiotics have been seen to affect the aura greatly and, although the damage eventually repairs itself once the drug has been withdrawn, the bioluminescence rarely recovers.

THE BRAIN AND THE AURA

More recent studies into the brain and how it functions have shed even more light on the great mystery of why we have psychic experiences at all.

Contained within the bony box of the skull is a complex mass of nerve cells called neurons and these are assisted by other cells known as neuroglia. The majority of these trillions of cells are contained within a layer of grey matter called the cerebral cortex, which neurologists believe to be the centre of consciousness and thought. The cells across this area are responsible for the processing of data received from the external world, by means of our five senses. Once processed, the data are then transferred to the internal regions of the cerebral cortex. Individuality is then created once the memory data have joined together with various other pieces of information from other parts of the brain, to form feelings, thoughts, images and ideas.

Although the information is processed by the brain's neurons through electrical impulses, how exactly these impulses become thoughts and feelings is still baffling to those researching in the field of neuroscience. One interesting scientific conclusion is that we have three brains as opposed to one, each one vastly different from the others in both structure and function. However, even though the three brains all appear significantly different, there is some sort of correspondence between them.

The first and oldest of the three brains is known as the reptilian brain and is responsible for our survival instincts, the hunter and fighter in us, and most probably the lower passions and emotions. The limbic system, the second part of the brain, is an interconnected system of brain nuclei and associated with basic needs and emotions; for example, hunger, pain, pleasure, sexual desire and instinctive motivation. This is located in the inner wall of each cerebral hemisphere and includes the brain system concerned with the sense of smell. The most recently evolved and third part of the brain is the cerebral cortex, believed to represent the clear divide between humans and animals, as the saying goes: 'Man knows, the animal knows, but man knows that he knows'. This is the reasoning part of the brain and the part that enables us to form ideas, create culture and learn new concepts.

Some psychologists believe that the human is in fact a twofold being consisting of the 'ego' or real self, as in Eastern philosophy, and an intuitive 'self'. Most psychologists believe that the ego is situated in the cerebral cortex, the newest part of the brain, and the intuitive self is associated more with the oldest part of the brain, which is referred to as the cerebellum, the unconscious, and the part of the brain responsible for dreams. In fact, some believe that the cerebellum is also responsible for paranormal experiences and is the part of the brain that controls the so-called 'trance' state. However, there are conflicting theories about this concept, and others researching the subject of the function of the brain believe that the cerebral cortex, in the right hemisphere of the brain, is in fact where psychic experiences originate.

Scientists in America also believe that they have identified the module in the brain in which God exists, and that many people suffering from temporal lobe epilepsy have spiritual experiences. Scientists all over the world are today endeavouring to understand the complexities of the brain, and to find out why many people claim to have paranormal experiences. Tests have shown that the electrical circuitry in the brain of a psychic or medium is somehow significantly interrupted when he or she is working, and a significant fluctuation in brainwave activity is also apparent when monitored by an electroencephalograph (EEG). Experiments were conducted using a computerised aura camera, whilst a psychic was also connected to an EEG. The results revealed an obvious correspondence of activity between the graph of the EEG and the computerised imagery of the aura camera, leaving very little doubt that brain activity did most definitely affect the polarity of the psychic's aura. However, some working in the field of metaphysics believe that it could be the other way round, and that it may be the fluctuation in auric polarity that affects the electrical activity in the brain. Whatever the conclusions, as I have previously said the brains of psychics are far from normal, and significant changes most certainly do occur in the overall activity of the electrical circuitry when they are practising their psychic skills.

CHAPTER SEVEN
PSYCHIC SELF-DEFENCE
AND THE AURA

Although most people are unaware of it, we are constantly being invaded and influenced by the thoughts created by minds past and present, and very often we can find ourselves overwhelmed by the forces of such thoughts, which either pull us into the mire of depression or even spur us on to the heights of greater fulfilment. I am not simply talking about such things as the hate, resentment and malice that might be directed at us by those who dislike us, but also about the subtle atmospheres we all experience from time to time in old buildings or even in specific geographical locations. However, some people are much more sensitive to these vibratory atmospheres than others. Nonetheless, regardless of whether or not one is sensitive, everyone is ultimately affected by the invisible forces that permeate the psychic space surrounding them; forces that often have the profound effect of flooding the mind with the emotions connected to the time they were first created.

Although the majority of psychic forces that are released into the atmosphere have no particular power behind them and were perhaps not originally created with the intention of influencing the minds of other people, there are certain individuals who do create such forces with the sole intention of influencing others for either good or ill.

It is of paramount importance that those working in the psychic field always remain mindful of the fact that they, more than anyone else, are susceptible to psychic invasion either from incarnate minds - that is, others working in the same field who are aware of the powers they possess - or perhaps from discarnate vagabonds roaming menacingly through the lower regions of the astral world. To a sceptic this most probably sounds extremely far-fetched and fanciful, but even those who have nothing whatsoever to do with psychic or metaphysical things need to take care, for they too may be the subject of psychic attack, regardless of whether or not they believe in this very real and yet dangerous phenomenon.

Even your innocent dislike of someone potentially has the power to produce a negative effect on that person's aura. However, should you persist in your dislike of them, in the long term that effect will return to you with increased force. In fact, there is an ancient Yogic precept that illustrates this phenomenon perfectly: 'Curses and blessings come home to roost'. Should you be in the habit of thinking jealous or even malicious thoughts about someone who does not deserve it, then your thoughts will most certainly rebound from his or her aura, and will then return to you having gathered force from the impact. In fact, we are all slaves to the thoughts we release into the atmosphere and are constantly creating our future environment. We are most certainly the architects of our own destinies by the way we think, and our mode of thinking affects our own personal energy field and eventually has an even greater effect on all those with whom we come into contact. We are constantly peopling our own private portion of space by the way we think. In fact, although something of a cliché, thoughts are living things. The stronger the thoughts the more energy we charge those thoughts with. The more energy present within our thoughts, the longer they persist in the psychic space. Our aura has the power to attract or repel both situations and people, and the mind is the common denominator. Therefore, in order to create a peaceful, loving environment it is necessary to think peaceful, loving thoughts. This is easier said than done in such a competitive world where everyone is intent on making a good life for themselves, frequently with a disregard for others. But this is the law of consequence - a universal law that is both right and just.

You may find yourself the focus of sustained intentional hate or jealousy, or perhaps simply at the receiving end of a spate of dislike from a work colleague or even a neighbour. If things have been going consistently wrong in your life for some time, it could be that you are the focus of a malicious psychic attack, the perpetrator of which may even have sufficient power to sustain it long enough to cause you physical as well as psychological pain. A great deal of nonsense is spoken about psychic self-defence and about what one ought and ought not to do. Although locating the actual source of the attack would make the method of protection more efficient, it is not absolutely necessary. The most important part is the actual belief that the psychic protection method you have created will work.

PSYCHIC SELF-DEFENCE
Method One
Each night before going to sleep, lie quietly on your bed with your eyes fixed on a certain spot on the ceiling. Begin to breathe rhythmically, slowly and deeply, with even inhalations and exhalations. Resist the temptation to blink, but when the eyes move out of focus slowly close them. Feel overwhelmed with a sense of tranquillity and peace. Create in your mind a beautiful pool of pulsating blue light, the kind of blue that colours a clear sky on a summer's day. Let this pool of clear blue light be full of movement, almost alive. See it very clearly in your mind, and allow it to expand slowly until it completely fills your room and surrounds you.

Across the surface of the pool of clear blue light create an equidistant golden cross, whose intersecting lines reach out to establish four points of contact at the circumference of the pool. In this way your sacred pool is sealed by the power of the equidistant cross. Now, see yourself lying at the centre of the pool and allow the blue light to surround you. Then physically extend your arms, and imagine yourself lying on the cross. Feel the golden rays emanating from the cross and passing through you. Do not permit your mind to wander even for a moment from this picture of yourself and the pool.

Feel yourself becoming submerged in the pulsating pool of clear blue light, and mentally say to yourself three times, 'This is the sacred pool and I am filled with the power of the golden cross and the mighty force of the universe will protect me. NO HARM SHALL COME TO ME.'

Recreate the sacred pool of light each night before you go to sleep, and eventually you should be free of malevolence. However, should you experience no change, then move on to the following psychic self-defence method.

Method Two
Sit in a relaxed position in a comfortable chair. Breathe slowly and deeply for a few moments, until the mind is quiet and serene.

In your mind create a curtain of blue light, beginning from the floor by your feet, all the way up to the ceiling above your head. Light up this curtain of blue with sparkling rays of silver, rather like currents of electricity flowing along a bare connection. Allow the curtain of blue light to overwhelm you, almost taking your breath away. Draw the blue light in through your nostrils and down into your body. In fact, fill your body completely with blue light.

Very slowly, change the curtain of blue light to red. Allow the red light to envelop you as completely as possible, and feel energised, vibrant and full of vitality. Feel the energies of the red light warm against your skin, and see its power burning its way through your aura, infusing it with strength and vitality. Feel the power of the red light inside your body, filling every part of your being with vitality and cleansing your entire aura in the process. Hold this imagery for a few moments longer, watching the red light moving through and around you, cleansing and revitalising your body and your mind.

Gradually change the red energy to a bright golden light. Allow the golden light to enfold you slowly. See it clearly in your mind, and quietly acknowledge the golden light as the most powerful universal force, and that this will always protect you against evil, jealousy and hate. Maintain this imagery for a few minutes before relaxing.

Remember not to allow your mind to drift from the visualisation even for one second, as this would merely defeat the whole object of this exercise.

Conclude the exercise by breathing rhythmically, ensuring that the inhalations and exhalations are evenly spaced and that you do not strain your breathing or make the exercise a labour. Continue breathing in this way for three to five minutes and open your eyes when you feel ready.

Not everyone can visualise in this way, but if you persevere with the exercise you will eventually derive great benefits from it, as well as feeling totally protected and cleansed.

Method Three
We have all been in the company of someone with an overbearing personality, making us feel nervous and intimidated. These sorts of people unwittingly tend to cause us to feel depleted and drained of energy, and although this may not be the usual definition of 'psychic attack', the effects on our nervous system are very much the same. People with overpowering personalities unknowingly tend to infiltrate our personal energy fields, and should we have no alternative but to be in the presence of such an individual on a regular basis (for example, in the workplace) then in order to maintain one's health something constructive must be done. Although there are innumerable methods of replenishing the nervous system, I have found the following exercise to be the most effective. It not only replenishes the levels of energy, but also has the psychological effect of 'closing the tap'.

* Sit comfortably with your eyes closed, making certain that the spine is straight.
* Following the breathing technique practised earlier (see pages 28 and 29), breathe rhythmically until the rhythm is fully established, making sure that the inhalations and exhalations are evenly spaced.
* Clasp your hands in front of you, and with your thumbs pulled apart (thus opening the tap) slowly breathe in, imagining streams of intense white light passing through the nostrils down into the solar plexus (a major nerve centre located at the pit of the stomach).
* Then, pressing your thumbs together (closing the tap), breathe out streams of grey light, expelling the negative energy from your body.

* Repeat the process for five to ten minutes and then relax.
* This exercise should be practised first thing in the morning and then again last thing at night.

The technique of using the thumbs as a means of opening and closing the energy tap produces a powerful psychological effect on the aura. Pulling the thumbs apart allows the inflowing energy unrestricted passage, and closing the thumbs on the exhalation allows only the negative energy to be discharged.

Once this method has been mastered successfully, you can then apply it when you are in the presence of someone who is sapping your energy. Simply clasp your hands comfortably in front of you for a few moments with your thumbs closed together. You don't even have to make it obvious to the person to whom you are talking. Your mind will have been psychologically programmed already, and the simple process of clasping yours hands in front of you will have the effect of sweeping the aura and closing the tap. The benefits of this are instantaneous.

CHAPTER EIGHT
DEVELOPING PSYCHIC
SKILLS

Before our prehistoric forebears evolved even the most rudimentary form of speech it is a commonly held view that they communicated their thoughts and feelings telepathically. In fact, one notable writer once said: "Man only developed speech so that he could lie!" Whether or not the latter is true, the fact remains that the mind is capable of much more than we realise, and by cultivating the aura and learning how to use it to its full advantage we can gain greater control of our lives, in more ways than one.

Today, more and more people are showing an enthusiastic interest in the paranormal and especially in the process of psychic development. Although everyone is psychic potentially, some people have a much greater propensity towards being psychic than others, and may even occasionally experience some form of rudimentary psychic skill. This sporadic paranormal ability is very often misleading and may even mistakenly lead the individual into believing that he or she is 'psychic'. By working on the faculties through the aura, you can learn to 'control' your psychic skills as opposed to their controlling you. Cultivation of the aura encourages the development of the faculties and helps to trigger latent psychic skills.

The safest and most effective way of encouraging psychic abilities is through meditation. However, meditation techniques vary and what suits one person may not necessarily be suitable for another. Each person's brain is uniquely structured and therefore functions differently to that of someone else. Some people have the ability to concentrate, whilst other people's minds are like butterflies, constantly flitting from one thing to another. Meditation is the process of focusing the mind on one particular thing to the exclusion of all else. Once effective meditation has been achieved, a corresponding effect is then produced on the person's aura, infusing it with delicate streams of either aquamarine or violet. These colours represent balance and awareness, and reveal that psychic developement has taken place.

CANDLE GAZING EXERCISE

Although strictly speaking meditation is a structured programme for training the mind to be more focused, the following exercise is a complete meditation process in itself, and may either be integrated into your daily meditation routine or used by itself. It is frequently used in yoga as a method of quietening the mind prior to meditation, but it is also an ideal tool with which to encourage the image-making faculty of the mind, particularly when an inability to visualise is experienced. Candle gazing is an ancient method of scrying and requires very little effort to achieve maximum results.

For this exercise you will require a lighted candle, some pleasant incense and a comfortable straight-backed chair.

Ensure that the lighting in the room is fairly subdued. Burn the incense to create a pleasant atmosphere, and then place the lighted candle approximately two feet away and as near to eye level as possible.

* Sit quietly, making sure that your chest, neck and head are in as straight a line as possible, with your shoulders thrown slightly back and your hands resting lightly on your lap.
* Breathe rhythmically for a few moments, ensuring that the inhalations and exhalations are evenly spaced.
* Move your gaze to the tip of the candle's flame and simply stare at it. Resist the temptation to blink or move your eyes away from the flame even for a moment.
* Don't try to focus your thoughts on anything in particular, just allow them freedom to come and go without any interference whatsoever.
* When you feel that you can no longer gaze at the flame, and your eyes begin to 'tear', close them very slowly and then gently place your hands over them. Within a few moments the after-image of

the flame will gradually appear in your mind's eye.

* Hold the after-image of the flame in your mind's eye for as long as you possibly can.

* Simply watch the after-image in your mind, and begin to breathe rhythmically, once again ensuring that the inhalations and exhalations are evenly spaced, and that you feel totally relaxed.

* You should begin to notice that with each inhalation the after-image grows stronger and more clearly defined.

* When the after-image begins to dissolve in your mind, slowly open your eyes, return your gaze to the flame, and then repeat the whole process again. In fact, in order to achieve maximum results, the exercise should be repeated four to five times each session.

If this technique is practised at least once a day over a period of four weeks, you should notice that the after-image of the flame starts to remain in your mind's eye much longer. This exercise stimulates the image-making faculty of the mind and encourages concentration and the ability to visualise. However, remember not to make it a labour or overuse the exercise, as this merely defeats the whole object of it.

CHAPTER NINE
HOW TO CULTIVATE
THE SENSES

The world in which you live your day-to-day life has a much greater influence on you than you might imagine. In fact, you are very much what your knowledge of this world makes you. You know this world by means of your five senses, and should one of these senses become defective for some reason or another then your knowledge of this world would naturally be less as a consequence of that defect. Although you might not realise it, your senses are being used every single moment of every day, and you are continuously seeing, hearing, touching, tasting and smelling the objects of the world around you. However, the majority of people have only a superficial encounter with the world about them, and so very often fail to register exactly what their senses are telling them.

As an example, you are most probably sitting comfortably whilst reading this book, and more than likely you have not given it a second thought. Why should you when it's something you frequently do every day? However, having drawn your attention to the fact that you are sitting comfortably, I bet you shifted your bottom slightly on the chair. The same thing applies to the fact that you are holding the book in your hands. I have now drawn your attention to it, making you aware of the book being held between your fingers. If I tell you to think of a grey elephant you immediately see a grey elephant in your mind's eye. If you are asked about the temperature in the room in which you are sitting, your senses automatically 'home in', so to speak, to register whether it is warm or cold in the room. In fact, throughout the day our senses are constantly moving from one to the other, when we're looking and being observant, listening intently to something, smelling particular fragrances, feeling the quality of a fabric, or even tasting a particular food. It's quite normal only to use the senses required to process data from whatever you are interested in at that particular moment - everybody does it! However, by cultivating our awareness and encouraging it to be more focused, we can develop a more heightened sense of the world around us. This produces incredible changes in the aura, making it more vibrant and intense. Once this transformation has been initiated fully, more positive vibrations will be registered in the aura. This will make you far more dynamic, regardless of what work you do.

To obtain maximum results from the following exercise, it is necessary to devote at least one hour each day to this part of the programme. It would be far too easy to dismiss the 'processing the senses' technique on the grounds that you think it is too simple and therefore would not help you to achieve anything. However, this exercise has been used for thousands of years by Native Americans as well as ancient Yogic Masters as a means of cultivating the senses.

PROCESSING THE SENSES EXERCISES
To help you with these exercises you will need to enlist the help of a friend, who should keep a record of the results.

Taste
* To put your sense of taste to the test, out of view your friend will need to select a variety of food samples and an assortment of drinks.
* Wearing a blindfold, taste the first sample of food, which may be anything from fruit to baking powder. Tell your friend what you think you are tasting and ask them to make a note of your answer.
* Experiment with as many samples of food and drink as you can, and at the conclusion of the experiment see how many you identified correctly.

Smell
* Now your friend will need to select a variety of different fragrant substances, ranging from perfume to washing-up liquid; in fact, anything with a distinct odour.

* Wearing a blindfold, as with the previous experiment see how many of the fragrances you can identify, ensuring a record is kept of the results.
* Take time with each fragrance and even mentally absorb it so that it can be fully established in your mind.

Touch
Primarily because we are touching objects most of the day, the sense of touch is perhaps the most underestimated of all the senses. The object of this exercise is to see how much information is gleaned from the article you are holding. Therefore, to ensure the information you give can be confirmed, the history of the articles used in the exercise should be known to the person with whom you are working.
* Wearing a blindfold, take the selected article in your hands, and feel all its qualities, i.e., its size, weight, texture, shape and even its temperature.
* Take your time in assessing and describing each quality and use as many fingers as possible in the exercise.
* Spend some time with the exercise and process as many different articles as possible, such as rings, brooches, watches, in fact, anything that will stimulate the image-making faculty.
* At the conclusion of the experiment, see how much of the information you have given can be confirmed.

Sight
Processing the sense of sight is perhaps the second most complex of sense exercises. It is more an experiment in 'observation' and is an exercise to cultivate your ability to process information coming into your brain through the sense of sight.

* Allow your friend to choose a room, preferably in his or her home, in which to seat yourself. Then, prior to putting on a blindfold, spend five minutes mentally scanning and making a mental picture of your surroundings.
* Once blindfolded, try to describe in detail everything you can remember about the room. Begin with the general layout of the

46

room, such as the positioning of the furniture and the location of doors and windows, and then move on to more detailed observations, such as the colour and pattern of the curtains and decor, the flooring and what kind of lighting was in the room, etc.
* Once again, at the conclusion of the exercise check to see how many of your recollections were correct.

Hearing

The processing of data through your sense of hearing is the other more complex exercise, also involving observation but this time through your ability to 'hear' things. The best results with this exercise are probably achieved outdoors where there are a greater variety of sounds.

* Blindfolded, sit in the garden or another place of your choice, and simply listen.
* Make a mental note of everything you can hear, such as cars passing by, dogs barking, children playing, people talking, the wind, birds singing - in fact, everything that your sense of hearing registers - and then share your observations with your friend.
* Spend a little longer with this experiment than the previous ones and be as meticulous as you can in your analysis of the individual sounds around you.

Regularly processing all five senses in this way helps to cultivate their overall efficiency, in just the same way that one would exercise the body to improve its power and strength. However, processing the senses should be integrated into a daily programme, including your chosen method of meditation, which will be covered later.

In time, your ability to sense the aura should develop and become more efficient with use.

CHAPTER TEN
DOWSING THE AURA

Once you are completely familiar with the aura and have become quite comfortable working with it, you are ready to really experience it with the use of different dowsing methods. Dowsing the aura has its uses, particularly when endeavouring to locate the extent of a person's aura and it will even help visually to pinpoint fragmentations and leakages. This is invaluable to someone working as healer and will help the practitioner to be specific when applying the healing process. Dowsing also helps to accustom you with the concept of 'energy', and even if you cannot 'see' the aura the dowsing process will at least nurture your sensitivity to it.

There are, in fact, two extremely effective methods of dowsing the aura: one using dowsing rods and the other using a pendulum.

Because the inner areas of the aura move in a spiralling motion, the use of a pendulum allows you to locate easily the points at which the major chakras connect to it. Although a sensitive is able to 'feel' the aura simply by moving his or her hands across the outside of a person's body and therefore does not require a pendulum or any other tools to establish where the auric radiations are exactly, a pendulum makes it more visual.

Dowsing rods may be obtained from most 'New Age' shops. Should you have difficulty in purchasing them they can easily be made from wire coat hangers. Simply unwind two coat hangers, cut them to equal lengths, and then bend each one into an 'L' shape, and there you have your dowsing rods. Although crudely made they will do the job just as well. These should be about 16 inches in length. Dowsing the aura with a pendulum is a little different to using dowsing rods and is probably a lot more interesting. Although almost anything can be used as a pendulum, I prefer to use a quartz crystal on a length of string. Use whatever you feel comfortable with.

DOWSING METHOD ONE - DOWSING RODS

For this experiment once again you will need to enlist the help of a very patient and understanding friend.

As I have previously explained, generally speaking the aura is more extensive at the back than it is at the front.

* Ask your friend to stand at one end of the room with their back to you.
* Position yourself at the opposite side of the room (or at least eight feet away.)
* Holding the dowsing rods gently in your hands, move slowly towards your friend, making sure that the rods are pointing towards them.
* The dowsing rods will indicate when you have reached your friend's aura by crossing over, giving visual proof of how far their aura extends into the space behind them.
* Now, repeat the process, only this time with your friend facing you, so that you can dowse the aura at the front.
* Once again, as soon as the dowsing rods have located the person's aura they will cross over. This time, however, you should notice that the aura at the front is not as great as at the back.

Further Experiment

* Once the dowsing experiment above has been completed, prepare to repeat the whole process again.
* This time, however, allow a few minutes of complete silence whilst your friend faces the wall waiting for the experiment to begin. Remain silent and allow the anticipation to build for as long as you can.
* Move the dowsing rods slowly towards your friend as before, and you should be amazed to see an incredible increase in their aura. This is because the anticipation of waiting in silence causes the protective antennae of the aura to extend further.
* Once your friend feels more comfortable and begins to relax, the aura at the back should then begin to decrease.

49

DOWSING METHOD TWO - PENDULUM

For this experiment you will need to ask your partner to lie on their back on the floor or bed, ensuring there is sufficient room for you to move freely around them.

* Once your partner is quite relaxed, allow the pendulum to hang loosely about two inches from their forehead.
* Move the pendulum very slowly in a zigzag manner, firstly to the throat, then to the chest, the stomach, the abdomen, and from the thighs along the legs to the feet.
* As you do this, watch the crystal closely for any involuntary or unusual movement and make a mental note of each instance.
* Now, retrace your route back along the body up to the head.
* Once back at your starting position, allow the crystal to remain suspended approximately two inches above the forehead for a minute or two.
* Although the tension in your arm is bound to produce some vibration in the crystal, by now you should have noticed some additional movement.
* Observe whether the crystal appears to be pulling in a particular direction, indicating exactly where on the body it wants to be.
* Once the pendulum has settled down (i.e., stopped pulling) it will begin to rotate slowly, either clockwise or anticlockwise. This movement indicates that a major chakra has been located, and the direction of the circular motion (clockwise or anticlockwise) reveals the exact polarity of its force.

Although traditionally chakras are located in a more or less vertical line from the crown of the head to the base of the spine, because we are all anatomically different their positioning is not always so clear cut. So do not mistakenly think that you have wrongly calculated their whereabouts, as your partner's chakras may be positioned differently.

Generally speaking, there is a significant variation in the polarity of each individual chakra but, as a consequence of a variety of influencing factors, most chakra systems tend to be either extremely sluggish or significantly out of sync. Either of these effects is nearly always produced by poor diet, stress, lifestyle and wrong thinking. A correctly aligned chakra system is nearly always found in a healthy, dynamic individual, and is mostly the result of good living, self-discipline and correct thinking.

A pendulum held close to the right side of a person usually moves in a clockwise motion, indicating positive polarity in the aura at that point. When it is held on the left side it should move in an anti-clockwise motion, indicating negative polarity. These movements are very often reversed in a person with poor health.

CHAPTER ELEVEN
THE AURA AND HEALING

The human body is permeated with an extremely intricate network of channels, the Hindu word for which is 'nadis'. The word nadi means 'nerve', only at a more subtle level, and it is along these nadis that energy flows from the major chakras to the organs of the physical body. The maintenance of the health in the physical body is solely dependent on the way in which energy freely and consistently moves along the nadis. Therefore, any restriction of energy movement produces a negative effect on the corresponding parts of the body, thus causing a breakdown in the overall health of the individual. Detailed studies of computerised imaging of the aura have shown that minute multicoloured flares of energy can be seen erupting at strategic points across the surface of the skin, and that these flares of energy more or less correspond with the 700 points charted through acupuncture, the ancient Chinese method of treating disease by inserting fine needles in the skin at specific points. When measured by the Russian electronic device, the tobiscope, these multicoloured flares of energy appear also to have a much higher electrical conductivity than at any other points on the body.

Before the development of the aura camera, even in its crudest Kirlian form, the phenomenon of the aura belonged to the world of fanciful ideas, supposition and conjecture. However, today incredible advancements have been made in the world of metaphysics, and now there is very little doubt at all that the aura is a scientific fact - a metaphysical phenomenon. Because the aura is luminous and semi-translucent, it is very difficult to perceive it in daylight, and so the aura camera makes it possible for it to be studied in great detail.

Following extensive studies in the early fifties into the biolumi-nescence of the body, Russian scientists were convinced that they had discovered the 'key' to making an accurate diagnosis of disease, and concluded that all diseases were visible in the aura long before they became apparent in the physical body. Bioluminescence is the production and emission of light by a living organism, and is thought to be the result of a chemical reaction during which chemical energy is converted to light energy. The word 'bioluminescence' originates from the Greek *bios* for 'living' and the Latin *lumen* meaning 'light'. Once photographed with the Kirlian camera disease became apparent through varying changes that appeared in the bioluminescence of the body. This procedure was an innovation at the time and was an inspiration to others working in the same field.

The scientists' extensive research into the bioluminescence of the human body led them to postulate that there is a 'bio-plasma body' interpenetrating the physical body. They further concluded that this bio-plasma body was a sort of 'etheric framework', or matrix on which the physical body is constructed, rather like the wire framework on which a sculptor moulds his clay. It seemed to the researchers that when the bio-plasma body sustained damage as a consequence of an inconsistent energy flow, a corresponding effect was produced in the overall structure of the physical body, manifesting as disease. A Kirlian photograph of the limbs of an amputee showed that although the person's leg was absent from the knee down the bio-plasmic image was still complete, and the outline of the amputated leg could still be seen. A similar phenomenon occurred with a photograph of a leaf that had been cut in half. The Kirlian photograph showed that the leaf was still whole, proving that the bio-plasmic structure was intact.

During the Russian experiments, a Kirlian image was taken of the hands of a well-known healer both before and during the healing application. The photographs revealed that an incredible change occurred in the flares of energy erupting from the healer's hands during the healing process, and also a powerful surge of energy was seen to pass from the healer's hands to his patient. A Kirlian photograph was also taken of the patient's aura both before and after the healing session, and on the conclusion of the healing application the patient's bioluminescence appeared to glow brightly as though it had been infused with energy. The

Russian experiments also showed that startling changes occurred to the patient's bioluminescence when healing was administered consistently over a long period of time, leading them to conclude that in most cases a cure could be successfully achieved. As the healing process was completely holistic, it was not necessary for the healer to administer the healing to one particular part of the body but simply to apply it to the area around the head and shoulders, maintaining that before the part could be healed the whole person must first be treated.

CHAPTER TWELVE
CHAKRAS - THE
WHIRLPOOLS WITHIN

The human organism is an electromagnetic unit of incredible power, assimilating and releasing energy, and is contained within its own spectrum of light and colour. This magnetic field, the aura, interpenetrates the physical body and also reaches out to integrate with other energies. Thus, to maintain perfect balance in the human organism, such power needs to be controlled, modulated, divided and evenly distributed throughout the body. This is the role of the chakras, which are like small electrical transformers, controlling the inflowing energy and then distributing it to the major organs of the physical body. As previously mentioned, although there are hundreds of minor chakras throughout the subtle anatomy, there are seven major chakras that are considered primary and these are to be found across the surface of the etheric tract in the spinal column, beginning at the base of the spine and finishing on the crown of the head. Each of these chakras performs a particular function and is responsible for the evolution of consciousness at its corresponding level.

Although all seven major chakras are potentially present at birth, it normally takes a full seven years for the entire chakra system to evolve fully. Thus, when a child emerges from its mother's womb only one chakra is fully active - the 'base chakra' at the bottom of the spine, which controls the autonomic nervous system, supervising the involuntary functioning of the body. The base chakra is also the one that instinctively encourages a baby's lips to seek its mother's breast. The consciousness of a newborn baby lives in the base chakra for 12 months, after which time the second chakra gradually begins to unfold, and so on, until all seven major chakras are fully formed at the age of seven. Up until this age a child's aura is completely untainted and it only begins to change when adults begin the process of training and chastising. Although a child is chastised long before this age, psychological programming only takes place when the chakra system is fully formed.

Chakras are symbolically represented by small lotus flowers, the petals of which increase as they ascend the spine. Because of the number of petals it possesses, the chakra situated at the crown of the head is symbolically represented by the 'Thousand Petal Lotus'. However, at this stage of evolution the crown chakra is dormant in the majority of people, and only awakens in those who attain a certain level of spiritual consciousness.

Only those who are making a serious study of the phenomenon of the aura and the bioluminescence of the human energy field will fully appreciate the connection between that and the chakra system. As previously established, the human organism comprises an incredible spectrum of colour and sound, integrated into a vast system of whirlpools of energy and light. As with the aura, the existence of the chakras can now be scientifically substantiated and their function supported using a similar photographic technique.

Although not absolutely essential, as a discipline and exercise in memory, it is worthwhile learning the original Sanskrit names of the chakras, as listed below:

Chakra	Anatomical Position
Muladhara	Base of the spine
Svadhisthana	Splenic centre
Manipura	Solar plexus
Anahata	Heart centre
Vishudda	Throat
Ajna	Between brows
Sahasrara	Crown of the head

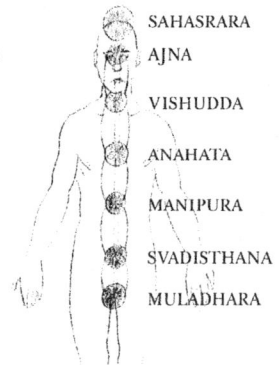

SAHASRARA
AJNA
VISHUDDA
ANAHATA
MANIPURA
SVADISTHANA
MULADHARA

DIAGRAM: ANATOMICAL POSITION OF THE CHAKRAS AND NADIS

NADIS

I have previously explained that the word 'nadi' means 'nerve', only at a more subtle level, and that it is along the nadis that energy flows from the chakras to the organs of the physical body. Now, though, it is important to comprehend the precise function of nadis and understand exactly what part they play in the manifestation of the aura.

When we have some form of recurring illness we might consult acupuncturist who, after making a detailed assessment of our symptoms, will treat the problem by inserting fine needles at strategic points across the surface of the skin. Blockages in the nadis cause disease of some form to manifest in the corresponding part of the body, and acupuncture breaks down these blockages and encourages the energy to flow freely once again, thus relieving the condition. The same principle applies to reflexology, the holistic process of locating all bodily points on the feet which is based on the assumption that health problems are reflected in crystallisation of energy in various points on the feet. The resultant crystals can be broken down by applying gentle massage to the appropriate areas in order to treat the condition. In acupuncture the channels along which energy flows are called meridians. I always think it is best to think of meridians as the tree trunks and the nadis as the branches, both integral parts in the manifestation and transportation of energy.

The physical body is a veritable network of channels along which energy is constantly moving, maintaining balance and sustaining life. However, there are three major nadis that are considered primary: Ida Nadi, Pingala Nadi and the central spinal channel, Sushumna Nadi. The Ida and Pingala nadis convey the female and male energies respectively, whilst Sushumna controls energy moving up the spine from the base chakra. Within the Sushumna nadi is the conduit for Kundalini (the Serpent Fire) dormant in the chakra at the base of the spine. Ida controls the female energy and is symbolised by the moon. Although located in the right side of the brain it passes through the left nostril. Pingala controls the male energy and is symbolised by the sun. Whilst it is located in the left side of the brain it passes through the right nostril. Both Ida and Pingala move energy from the base chakra to the brow chakra, and they coil around Sushumna in a serpentine fashion, connecting each chakra en route.

The yogic method of alternate nostril breathing is an excellent way to encourage balance and maximise the effects of Ida and

57

Pingala energies. This method of Pranic breathing is also an effective way of restoring equilibrium to the subtle anatomy. It is also an efficient way of alleviating stress and anxiety, particularly after a hard day at work.

ALTERNATE NOSTRIL BREATHING EXERCISE

* Sit comfortably, ensuring that your back, chest and neck are in as straight a line as possible, with your head and shoulders thrown slightly back.
* Place the tip of your right thumb lightly against the right nostril and the ring and little fingers lightly against the left. The index and middle fingers should be together and resting on the Ajna chakra, applying light pressure between the brows. This pressure should be maintained throughout the exercise.
* Exhale deeply and slowly through both nostrils.
* Close the right nostril by pressing the thumb against it. Slowly and quietly inhale deeply through the left nostril.
* Keep the right nostril closed and now apply pressure to the left nostril so that both nostrils are closed. Remain in this position for a count of three.
* Release the pressure on the right nostril, but ensure that the left nostril remains closed.
* Now, exhale slowly through the right nostril.
* Without pausing, immediately inhale through the same nostril - that is, the right nostril - whilst keeping the left nostril closed.
* When the breath is complete, close both nostrils for a count of three.
* Now release the left nostril, but keep the right nostril closed. Exhale slowly through the left nostril.
* Then, still keeping the right nostril closed, inhale slowly through the same nostril, that is, the left nostril.
* Close both nostrils for a count of three.
* Repeat the exercise for approximately five minutes, or for as long as you feel comfortable. Remember not to strain your breathing or make it a labour, as this merely defeats the object of the exercise.

Alternate nostril breathing techniques vary from teacher to teacher. For example, if you feel comfortable the count of three may be increased, or you may simply pause for a moment instead of counting. Read the instructions through a few times to fix the method firmly in your mind. As well as promoting calmness and serenity, alternate nostril breathing encourages perfect balance through the nadis, and should therefore be practised every day.

STIMULATING THE AURA AND CHAKRAS

There is nothing worse than having to attend an important meeting when you are feeling out of sorts and completely lacking in energy. Although rhythmic breathing (see page 23) is an extremely effective way of revitalising the body, sometimes the very process of slow and deep breathing can itself be a chore, particularly if you haven't even got the energy to do this. To some this will sound a little paradoxical, but believe me, only those who have experienced this will know exactly what I mean - absolutely no energy to breathe!

Hand Rotating Exercise for Energy Manipulation

This exercise requires the co-operation of a partner, on whom the treatment can also be applied.

* Lie flat on your back in a comfortable position with your eyes closed. Just relax as completely as you possibly can, not thinking of any one particular thing, but just allowing thoughts to come and go.
* Your partner should kneel comfortably beside you and place one hand on your forehead and the other hand on your solar plexus. The hands should remain in this position until your partner feels them becoming warm, at which point they should be withdrawn.

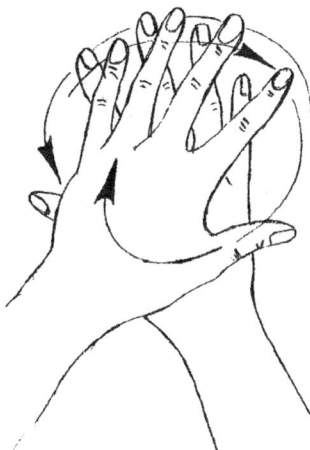

Rotating Hands

* Now your partner should place his or her left hand over your forehead, without touching it, at a distance of approximately 1in (2.5cm) away from it. Their right hand should then be placed over the left hand, again without touching it and approximately one inch away. The fingers should be spread apart on both hands.

* The healing process should be initiated by very slowly moving the left hand in a circular, clockwise motion, and moving the right hand over the left hand, in a circular, anticlockwise motion.

* This hand rotation should be maintained at a slow, steady pace for at least one minute and the hands should not be allowed to touch each other.

* Without stopping the hand rotation, the treatment should be slowly moved to the throat area and maintained for approximately one minute.

* Now the hands should move to the area of the heart where the same process should be repeated.

* Remember, the movements of the hands are of paramount importance, in order to create movement in the subtle energies of the aura.

* Maintaining the rotation, the hands should now be slowly and carefully moved to the area just below the left side of the ribcage, remaining there for one minute.

* The treatment should then be transferred to the area slightly above the naval, again maintaining the slow rotation of the hands for a period of approximately one minute.

* Finally, the continuously rotating hands should be moved slowly down to the lowest part of trunk and the treatment maintained for a further minute.

*This first part of the treatment should take eight to ten minutes.

* Now your partner should rest his or her left hand on your forehead, and right hand on your solar plexus and maintain this position as they intuitively determine which colour should be used in the second part of the treatment.

* The choice of colours is made by your partner by mentally flicking through the colours of the spectrum, and stopping at the one that seems to be most apparent. This probably sounds more difficult than it actually is. In fact, once your partner has

concluded the first part of the treatment he or she should have become closely attuned to your personal energies, and should just 'know' which colour is required in the process.

* Once the appropriate colour has been selected, your partner should commence the hand rotating process, beginning with the forehead as before.

*This time, however, your partner should endeavour mentally to envelop you in the chosen colour, whilst moving their constantly rotating hands slowly from your head down to your feet, without pausing at the previous treatment areas.

* Once the feet have been reached, the same route should be followed along the body back to your forehead.

* Once this procedure has been repeated twice, you should then lie on your front, and your partner should apply the same process along the back of your body.

Not only does hand rotation have an invigorating effect on the aura, it also encourages the movement of Prana in the subtle anatomy. This treatment stabilises the aura and helps to repair any damage or fragmented areas in it.

Once you have received the treatment, in order to enable you to become accustomed to this process of energy manipulation you should then apply it to your friend. The more you practise the above method, the stronger and more efficient your ability will become. You may even feel that the process can be modified a little to make it more effective and more suited to the way you work.

As a holistic healing method, this process is extremely effective in the treatment of respiratory, stomach or digestive problems, as well as debilitating spinal problems. It has an analgesic effect in cases where pain is quite severe and encourages a more serene bodily feeling.

Apart from the physiological benefits, the hand rotating method of energy manipulation stimulates the chakras and promotes a more consistent flow of Prana throughout the entire chakra system and in the aura.

Please note: The rotating hand method is also used further on in the book.

CHAPTER THIRTEEN
THE AURA AND COLOUR

All those now clichéd biblical sayings - 'in the pink', 'green with envy', 'feeling blue', 'red with anger' - are references to the aura and how it reflects a person's many different emotions. A coward is frequently referred to as 'yellow', and there is nearly always 'darkness' around someone who is not a good person. No sooner are you able to 'see' the aura than a whole new world opens up before you, allowing you to 'perceive' things as they really are.

My mother used to say to me, "Sometimes it's better not to know!" and I am now beginning to realise that she was most probably right. We humans are insecure enough without possessing the ability to perceive the reality of things. Having been psychic since I was a child, I am not too sure whether possessing that ability has made me insecure, or whether my insecurity has contributed in some way to my being psychic. Of one thing I am quite certain, however, which is that psychic skills most certainly amplify one's insecurities, and whilst the ability to 'see' the aura can be quite advantageous it can also cause disappointment by allowing us sometimes to see that those whom we thought really loved us do not love us after all.

When there is a strong attraction between two people, as well as the obvious physical attraction 'something else' takes place, only at a more subtle level. Love is an emotion that is quite difficult to define. We know only too well how love makes us feel, particularly when it is reciprocated, but actually to define it is more difficult than we realise. When people talk about falling in love with someone, we frequently hear them say, "There was some kind of chemical attraction." In many ways this is true. When we fall in love there is an exchange of energy, passing from one to the other, and the auras of those who have been 'smitten', so to speak, suddenly blend to become one complete kaleidoscopic display.

The auras of two people very much in love are seen to be awash with an extremely delicate shade of pink, and the energy radiating from each becomes perfectly synchronised and totally in tune. A similar process takes place when two people feel strongly that they have met before, even though they know they have not. "A kindred impulse their spirits sway" said mystic and writer, Maurice Maeterlink, when describing the phenomenon of such an affinity between two people. Love and devotion have their own individual auric colours, but collectively they display varying shades of pink and translucent red. When a person has a general love of all things in nature, however, they have bright translucent green through their aura. As mentioned earlier, the aura of a jealous or envious person also has shades of green, but it is often seen with flashes of dark red through it.

The world we live in has a greater influence on our lives than we might imagine. In fact, we are who we are as a result of the knowledge we have of this world. As discussed earlier, we know the world in which we live by means of our five senses, and if one of these senses is defective then our knowledge of the world would naturally be less as a direct consequence of that defect. Although our five senses are constantly operating, and we see, hear, touch, taste and smell the objects of the world around us, we do not realise what complex processes of consciousness are actually involved in our 'knowing' the world. Nor do the majority of people comprehend that we know only a minute part of what there is to be known about the world around us. For example, let us consider our knowledge of the world through the faculty of 'sight'. What is actually meant when we say 'we see' an object? It simply means that our eyes respond to the vibrations of light that are thrown off from the surface of the object, and that our consciousness translates those vibrations into ideas of form and colour. However, what we normally see is only the front or facing part of the object, never the whole.

To comprehend this concept more fully we must have an understanding of light. What exactly is 'light'? Light is fundamentally a vibration in the ether and, in accordance with the frequency and amplitude of the vibration, a colour is then produced. The sun throws off bundles of vibrations of various rates, and these bundles are called 'white light'. If we place a prism of glass in the path of a ray of white light, the particles of glass break down each bundle into its constituent vibrations; once these are registered by the retina of our eyes, they formulate in our consciousness that sense of 'colour'. We can normally see seven colours and these, together with their various shades and mixtures, make up the many colours of the world in which we live. However, the colours that we can see are not the only colours that exist. We can only see the colours to which our eyes respond and that response is very limited. In the colour spectrum we can see red to blue and then violet. Very few people can actually see any indigo, because of the frequency of its vibration, which tends to be outside our normal range of vision. Through modern scientific developments we now know that below the red of the spectrum and above the violet, there exist infrared and ultraviolet rays that our eyes cannot normally see, but if we could see them this world would have a completely different meaning to us.

Our sense of hearing is similarly affected. There are in fact sound waves above and below our normal range of hearing, and by developing the faculties it is possible to become aware of a new sequence of frequencies of both vision and sound.

The interpretation of the individual colours in the aura can only really be considered when there is an understanding of what they mean when appearing with another colour. For example, orange can be an indication of someone's warmth and strong willpower, but when orange appears with a darker shade of red it denotes cunning and the love of power over other people. Another example is green. Grass green by itself can be an indication that someone is cheerful and fairly well balanced, but when it appears with a reddish brown it denotes selfishness and slyness. Lots of things need to be considered before making an assessment of someone's aura. The shade, clarity and accompanying colours have to be carefully considered before any conclusions are drawn. For these reasons, and to give you a clearer understanding of auric colours, I have made a list of the various colours and their combinations.

SOME AURIC COLOUR COMBINATIONS

Pure Yellow:	Spiritual Intellect
Light Yellow:	Higher Thought
Dark Dirty Yellow:	Selfish, Jealous, Suspicious
Orange:	Energetic, Strong Willpower
Clear Orange:	Sociable, Extrovert
Bright Orange:	Ambitious, Strong Willpower
Golden Orange:	Self-control, Intellectual
Orange with Brown:	Lack of Ambition, Careless
Orange with Red:	Love of Power over Others
Jade Green with Pink:	Tolerance, Politeness
Green with Brown:	Selfishness, Deceit
Emerald Green with Blue:	Healing, Compassion
Clear Red:	Vitality, Energetic, Restless
Bright Clear Red:	Materialistic, yet Generous
Very Dark Red:	Low Motives, Selfishness
Cloudy Red:	Greed, Cruelty
Dull Smoky Red:	Lower Animal Passion
Dull Red with Black:	Fear, Anxiety
Infrared:	Psychic of a Low Nature
Dark Muddy Crimson:	Impure Sensuality
Deep Scarlet:	Lust, Animal Passion
Scarlet with Flashes of Black:	Malicious Hate
Flashes of Scarlet:	Anger, Temper, Rage
Pink:	Maternal Love, Sympathy, Loves Animals
Clear Delicate Pink:	Divine Compassion
Salmon Pink:	Universal Love
Rose Pink:	Joyousness of Spirit
Pure Rose:	Highest Form of Human Love, Devotion
Rose with a Flash of Lilac:	Devoted Affection
Bright Blue:	Confidence, Loyalty, Sincerity
Blue with Lavender:	High Thoughts, Religious
Clear Blue with Lavender:	Spiritual
Clear Light Blue with Sparks of White Light:	Spiritual Unfoldment

Deep Royal Blue:	Faith, Spiritual
Blue with Black:	Religious with Fear
Blue with Reddish Brown:	Religious, Selfish
Murky Brown:	Miserly
Dull Reddish Brown:	Avarice, Greed
Blue with Flashes of Red:	Religious Cunning
Green with Flashes of Brown:	Jealousy, Deceit
Bright Brown with Blue:	Meditative
Aquamarine with Yellow:	Spiritual, Intellectual
Grey with Flashes of Black:	Evil, Black Arts
Green and Grey:	Depression, Jealousy
Lemon with Flashes of Blue:	Spiritual Aspirations
Violet with Flashes of Blue:	Mediumistic, Psychic
Deep Violet and White:	Healing, Spiritual

Remember, these colours are merely to give you an idea and a better understanding of exactly what the colours in the aura mean. You should create your own colour chart by making a detailed analysis of what you think the colours mean. Your own interpretation is more important and will help you when making your overall assessment of the colours you have seen.

THE AURA AND THE COLOURS IN OUR ENVIRONMENT
It is quite amazing to think that the colours around us and even the colours we wear affect and influence the way we eat. For example, people who like to wear red do tend to like their food and very often eat far too much. Although red is energy building, it also stimulates the appetite and so is very useful when trying to encourage someone recovering from illness to eat. Yellow produces the opposite effect on the appetite and has a tendency to suppress it and is therefore a useful aid when trying to lose weight.

The concept of colour and how it influences our lives is by no means new and was in fact known to the Ancient Egyptians who used colour therapy to treat maladies of both the body and the mind.

The colours around us do infiltrate our personal energy fields.

For instance, the colours we like to wear are very often the colours that already saturate our auras and ones that we therefore do not need about us. Also, the colour arrangements in our homes have more of an effect on our minds than we might imagine. Certain colours may suit you but may not necessarily be suitable for the rest of your family, and may even encourage confrontation, anger and general disharmony in the home. One does not require much of an imagination to understand exactly what it is like to enter a room with a dismal decor, finished off in blacks and greys and other such depressing shades. Remaining in such a room for any length of time would only succeed in producing a corresponding effect on your mind, making you restless and depressed. On the other hand, bright and happy colours would also affect your mind by uplifting it and encouraging it to be happy and bright, just like the colours themselves.

Because children's auras are comparatively untainted by the experiences of the physical world, children are much more receptive to the vibrations of colour than their parents. Even the colour of the food they eat influences their minds and, quite aside from the nutritional content of the food you lay before them, the colour can either infuse them with calmness and tranquillity, or foster aggression and misbehaviour. Thus, just as thoughts and emotions produce an effect on the aura, it is also significantly affected by the food we eat.

Different types of food produce different colours in the aura. A person on a strictly non-meat diet will have a delicate shade of pink through his or her aura, whilst someone who eats meat will have an aura of varying shades of murky red. If our eating habits remain the same, the colours produced by the food we eat infuse the aura and become an integral part of our character and general make-up.

Although the colours in the aura generally change with every passing thought and feeling, there is a predominant part of the aura that represents our true character, and it is this that is greatly influenced by our habits and the environment in which we live. Although the other colours that make up the aura are transitory and undergo innumerable changes during our lifetime, the predominant aura is 'the real you', so to speak, and really only changes if you undergo some profound spiritual metamorphosis that causes your way of thinking to change completely.

Consequently, the ultimate development of the aura is holistic and covers a broad spectrum of your life, from the way you think to what you eat. If the aura appears vibrant and healthy, you can rest assured that the individual within it is also the same.

Colour is fundamental in the maintenance of the health of the physical body, and the correct balance of colour in the aura is of paramount importance. Therefore, when endeavouring to polarise and establish equilibrium in the aura, the diet as well as correct thinking must be considered collectively. We all know only too well how a walk in the countryside makes us feel, particularly when we are depressed or just out of sorts. Although the fresh air is invigorating, the varying colour combinations of nature infuse our auras with streams of vitality, producing and maintaining total balance and harmony. The powerful rays of green generate an incredible effect on our minds and promote a more stable energy flow throughout the chakra system.

CHAPTER FOURTEEN
CHECKING OUT
YOUR BALANCE

In view of the stresses, strains and worries of modern-day living, there is little wonder why the majority of us are out of balance in one way or another. Apart from meditation, correct diet and good living, there are really no other ways of maintaining balance in the subtle anatomy. In theory, a well-balanced aura will produce a corresponding effect on the chakra system, and paradoxically a well-balanced chakra system will produce the same effect on the aura. We are more or less in a catch-22 situation, as one will affect the other regardless of which way you approach it.

Let's take a look at the overall balance of the subtle anatomy. To do this it is important to ascertain just how effectively balance is maintained in the chakra system. This will give you a fairly good idea of what level of balance is maintained in your aura, and then you can decide what measures should be taken to encourage equilibrium in the entire subtle anatomy.

CHAKRA BALANCE CHECKING EXERCISE
For this experiment you will need to enlist the help of another person.

* Stand up straight, with your left hand by your side and your right arm extended in front of you.
* Ask your partner to push your extended arm downwards gently, using one hand, but resist their pressure sufficiently to clarify how much strength you possess in your arm. You will need to know this for purposes of comparison later.

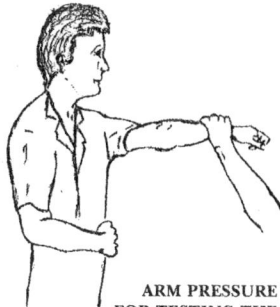

ARM PRESSURE
FOR TESTING THE
CHAKRAS

* Now rest your arm for a moment.
* Repeat the process but this time, whilst your partner is applying pressure to your right arm, place your left hand over your forehead, i.e. over your brow chakra and note any changes in the strength of your right arm.
* Rest your arm again.
* Repeat the process and this time place your left hand gently on your throat, again noting any changes to the resistance in your right arm.
* Rest your arm again.
* Repeat the process again, only this time place your left hand on your heart centre, again observing any change in the resistance of your right arm.
* Continue to apply the same process to the remaining chakras (see page 56 for positions), working your way through the whole chakra system, from the brow centre to the base of your spine.

The purpose of this exercise is to identify any sign of weakness when pressure is applied to your right arm, as this will indicate particular chakras that are not quite balanced. Chakra imbalance is not a permanent or serious condition, so there is no cause for concern.

In addition to enabling you to determine the condition of each chakra, this simple experiment also gives a good indication of the overall health of the aura. In the same way that weakness in the right arm is an indication that the chakra is not quite balanced, a feeling of strength in the right arm when pressure is applied is a clear indication that it is well balanced and correctly polarised.

Anyone who is extremely intuitive should have a fairly well-balanced brow chakra, and a person who is sympathetic and a good listener should have a well-balanced throat chakra. In fact, the mediumistically inclined person should find that both of these chakras are well balanced. The brow chakra is associated with the image-making faculty of the brain and is responsible for the psychic skill of 'seeing' or clairvoyance. The throat chakra is connected to the auditory system and is responsible for the mediumistic ability of 'hearing'. However, people whose brow and throat chakras are particularly active are not necessarily psychic. For instance, a highly skilled doctor who is extremely good at his or her job is usually very intuitive and is frequently able to assess a patient's condition very quickly. Intuitive skills are frequently seen in the dedicated policeman who nearly always goes on his or her 'gut' feeling to apprehend the perpetrator of a crime. Teachers who love their job of teaching also develop the faculties suitable for the work they do. People who devote their lives to caring for the sick or elderly, such as nurses, doctors and other care workers, usually have extremely well-developed heart chakras, and to be in their presence is very often healing in itself. In fact, the chakras that correspond with the job that you do develop quite naturally so long as you enjoy your work. The creative person nearly always functions in the brow, throat and heart chakras, making them imaginative and passionate about their craft. By using meditation to maintain balance in the chakra system it is possible to encourage the inherent qualities in each individual chakra to develop. Once the chakras have been correctly polarised, latent talents begin to surface, and the things you have only ever dreamed of doing may become a reality.

There are many ways of stimulating activity in the chakras, but the following exercise not only helps to infuse the chakras with vitality and power, but also causes a general feeling of well being. It has the effect of almost 'washing' one's aura with a powerful surge of energy, thus heightening general awareness.

For the exercise you will need a piece of amethyst crystal and a piece of clear quartz crystal, both small enough to hold comfortably in your hands. Amethyst, the spiritual stone, possesses calming qualities that affect the emotions and the nervous system, and it also heightens spiritual awareness. Clear quartz is an energy enhancer, increasing the energy in anything placed close to it, and it has the effect of clearing the mind and sharpening the senses. The combination of amethyst and clear quartz has a cleansing effect on the aura and encourages equilibrium throughout the entire subtle anatomy. (For a more detailed description of the different crystals and their uses, see Chapter 24.)

AURA AND CHAKRA CLEANSING EXERCISE

* Make sure you are sitting comfortably with your back straight.
* Take the piece of amethyst in your right hand and the clear quartz in your left, and sit quietly with your eyes closed and both hands on your lap.
* Remain in this position until your mind has become quiet.
* Then place your right hand, holding the piece of amethyst, gently on top of your head, and place your left hand, holding the piece of clear quartz, at the base of your spine.
* Remain in this position until you feel the temperature change in your right hand. (on top of head).
* Now swap the positions of your hands, placing your left hand (with the quartz) on top of your head, and your right hand (with the amethyst) at the base of your spine.
* Continue repeating the exercise until both hands have rested on the head at least ten times.
* Sit quietly for a further ten minutes with your eyes closed, allowing the energy to circulate around your body. If you have practised the exercise correctly you may feel your spine, forehead and hands tingling. You may also experience a feeling of disorientation and some light-headedness, as though you have breathed in fresh mountain air. This feeling will pass within a few moments.

There are, in fact, many benefits to be gained from this 'infusing' method. It is also effective in promoting calmness and serenity, and in easing pain.

Twenty minutes after you have completed this exercise repeat the arm pressure exercise described earlier in this chapter and note down any significant changes in the results. If you can see a marked improvement in your 'sluggish' chakras there will be little need for you to use any other method of chakra activation, unless of course you do not feel comfortable with this particular one.

NB: The temperature change should only occur in the hand on top of head, but it may happen in both hands.

CHAPTER FIFTEEN
CREATING THE RIGHT
ATMOSPHERE

The majority of psychics see the aura as a vaporous luminous cloud surrounding the entire body. In fact, the aura extends from two feet to three feet outwards in all directions from the body. It does not terminate abruptly, but gradually fades until it disappears completely and really extends quite a distance beyond this visible point. Its bioluminescence is a display of constantly moving colours, each representing a different aspect of the individual's being, from the emotional to the spiritual. The various colours of the aura are created by the person's mental, physical and spiritual states, and the atmosphere around the body is actually a blueprint of the individual's true nature. Even the non-psychic person cannot fail to be affected by another person's aura, and misery or joy, malevolence or spirituality, will either attract or repel them. Of course, circumstances may leave you with no option but to work in an unpleasant atmosphere alongside work colleagues with whom you have nothing at all in common, and who constantly make you feel tense and unhappy. Working in such an environment for any length of time will eventually have a negative effect on you and will, in the long term, be detrimental to your psychological well being. Although you may not be in a position to change your work colleagues, you do have the power to create a more conducive atmosphere by infusing your own aura with more vitality and, in so doing, take the first steps to reversing negative vibrations to positive ones. All that it takes is a few minutes of your time each day.

At the end of a hard and very stressful day at work the aura looks dull and lifeless, and when photographed with a Kirlian camera it appears fragmented and lacking in vitality. However, after something to eat and a good night's sleep, the aura's bioluminescence is replenished with its glow and vitality more or less restored. The whole process of revitalising the aura is easily achieved with a simple breathing and visualisation exercise, which will also sooth the discomfort of a stressful headache.

REVITALISING EXERCISE
* Sit in a comfortable chair for five or ten minutes, until you are quite relaxed and the mind is quiet.
* Then shake your hands vigorously until you can feel them tingle.
* Place your fingertips gently on your solar plexus and breathe slowly and deeply.
* Once you have regulated your breathing, take a slow, deep breath and imagine that you are breathing in a stream of intense white light through your nostrils, down into your solar plexus, and out into your fingertips.
* Hold that breath and slowly move your fingertips to your forehead, placing them gently between your brows.
* Now breathe out slowly and imagine that you are breathing the intense white light out through your fingertips, filling your head completely with it.
* When your breath has been fully expelled, pause and return your fingertips to your solar plexus.
* Now breathe the white light into your fingertips once again.
* Repeat the process, but this time move your fingertips slowly to the throat area.
* Expel all your breath, visualising the intense white light streaming through your fingertips and filling your throat with vitality and energy.
* When your breath has been fully expelled, return your fingertips to your solar plexus.
* Repeat the process, only this time move your fingertips slowly to the heart area, flooding the heart centre completely with intense white light.
* When your breath and the intense white light have been fully expelled, return your fingertips slowly to the solar plexus.
* Repeat the process, only this time carry the intense white light to the genital area.

* Once again breathe the intense white light out through your fingertips, flooding that area completely with vitality and energy.
* When your breath has been fully expelled, breathe in and out fairly quickly, ballooning your cheeks, and blowing through your lips with each exhalation.
* At the same time, sweep your open hands up and down the front of your face, chest and stomach areas. Do this four or five times.
* Then sit quietly for five minutes, imbibing the circulating energy which will appear to be vibrating through your whole body.

This is an extremely invigorating exercise, and one that you will find beneficial for stimulating the main chakras and infusing the aura with waves of Pranic energy. However, to gain the greatest benefits from it the exercise should be practised morning and evening.

Although it is believed that a healthy, well-balanced person should have a correctly vibratory-aligned chakra system with alternated movements, this may not always be the case, simply because the chakras do change polarity through the day, particularly when subjected to stress and disharmony. When this happens there is a noticeable change in the aura, causing some depression and sudden feelings of disorientation.

A stressful day at work can also be eased by hydrating the body with a glass of cold water charged with Prana.

WATER CHARGING - METHOD ONE
For this water-charging process you will need an empty glass and a glass of ice cold water. The process is quite simple:
* Pour the water from one glass to the other, backwards and forwards, for about one minute until the water is bubbly and appears to sparkle.
* Sip the water until only half a glass remains.
* Repeat the whole process of pouring the water from one glass to another until the water seems to 'come alive'.
* Drink the remaining water and then relax in a comfortable chair with your eyes closed. You should feel a tingling sensation

beginning in your stomach and then moving gradually all over your body.

For a surge of energy during the day, it is useful to drink some charged water mid-morning instead of having a cup of coffee.

Remember, visualisation is an integral part of the breathing exercise, and it is a good idea to experiment with different colours to see which colour affects you most.

Water can also be charged with vitality by introducing colour filters into the process. All colours have their own potent healing properties, and by using the appropriate coloured filter a glass of tap water can be easily transformed into a potent vessel of vitality. A glass of water charged in this way will have an immediate effect on the aura by infusing it with the appropriate colour ray.

First of all you will need several A4 pieces of acetate, one each of the different colours of the spectrum. These should be easily obtainable from any art shop.

Roll each piece of coloured acetate to make a tube wide enough to cover a drinking vessel and then sellotape or staple it securely together.

WATER CHARGING - METHOD TWO

* Place the appropriate coloured filter over a glass of water and leave it standing on a window ledge in the sunlight for half an hour. Should you be feeling lethargic and out of sorts, charge two glasses of water, one using a blue filter and the other using a red one. Blue is a natural healing colour that will revitalise the aura, and red will encourage energy and strength.

* Drink half of the contents of each glass, and then return the filtered vessels to the window ledge.

* Sit comfortably with your eyes closed for ten minutes, breathing rhythmically until the mind is quiet and serene, but taking care not to fall asleep.

* Consume the remainder of the contents of each glass, and then rest for a further ten minutes, again breathing rhythmically and ensuring that serenity of the mind is maintained.

* Feeling totally refreshed you can then go about your daily

routine.

Many people would probably dismiss these methods as being too simplistic to work. However, water charging has been used for thousands of years as an effective means of revitalising the body and maintaining health and balance. It must be noted, though, that maximum results will only be achieved when taken seriously and used on a regular basis.

CHAPTER SIXTEEN
FOCUSING THE POWERS
OF THE MIND

Most people live out their daily lives completely unaware of the powers that lie within them. A working person often experiences the day's routine almost mechanically, having gone through the same things day in, day out, for years. Regardless of whether they are more or less content or completely dissatisfied with their lives, the majority of people are ignorant of the fact that there are powers within their minds that, if channelled and released, could transform both themselves and their lives completely.

The poor man only dreams of being wealthy, thinking that riches are far beyond his reach; the weak and sickly person wishes for good health and strength; and the unhappy person hopes and prays for happiness. Most people live lives of hopes, wishes and dreams without possessing the knowledge that they could be in control of an inner power that is far greater than all these things.

It is easy to understand why anyone would find it difficult to think in a positive way when they encounter one problem after another, pushing them further and further into a state of despair. It is all very well to be told, "Be positive", but when you lack confidence you are consequently unable to think positively about your life. A person lacking in confidence and motivation has most probably spent a lifetime creating the fragile foundations on which his or her life is built. Thus, being able to transform a life that is uncertain and weak into one that is positive and strong seems a near impossibility.

Once a person's negative habits have been allowed to crystallise internally, they will gradually solidify in external situations and circumstances. Changing the habits of a lifetime is extremely difficult, but certainly not impossible.

The aura of a person who has spent a lifetime thinking

negatively about his or her life will send out negative signals to all those with whom they come into contact. A successful person does not become successful by being weak or negative. On the contrary, success is achieved through determination, right thinking and a positive attitude. Learning to focus the mind encourages the aura to send out positive signals, thus attracting opportunity and success.

When you are worried or anxious about something that is generally impairing the quality of your life, you probably find some comfort in sitting and relaxing for a few moments, quietly turning the problem over in your mind and exploring all the ways in which your predicament might be resolved. But, more often than not, somewhere along the line the imagination takes control, creating emotions that eventually convince you that things are definitely going to get worse. There is far more truth in the old saying 'You will worry yourself into an early grave' than you might imagine. It therefore makes sense that if it is possible to worry yourself into the grave the same principles must conversely apply to thinking your way to good health, happiness and success.

Although somewhat clichéd, 'thoughts are living things', and we are pulled along by the thoughts and desires that we have previously set in motion. However, when struggling in the mire of self-created despair and panic, the only way to free yourself from such negative conditions is to develop the self-realisation that these dark emotions have no real connection with your problems other than the connection you yourself make with them.

Worrying about situations and events that have not yet happened quite often hastens their approach and makes the thinker vulnerable and more susceptible to other, similar situations and events.

The way forward is to create new images in the imagination and to set these free, rather like large, helium-filled balloons floating off into space. You must create more than one image, however - don't forget that you have probably taken a lifetime to flood your life with worry and despair, so the first move forward must be with the positive realisation that within you there exists the power that can now set you free.

Those of you who have made a study of meditation and explored the possibilities of mind power will know that the electrical impulses produced by the brain change somewhat when certain meditative states are reached. These electrical impulses can be measured by connecting the meditator to an electroencephalograph (EEG), which measures and records the cyclic changes of electricity that occur in the brain during meditation. This offers conclusive evidence that meditation is capable of producing measurable changes in the brain.

A deep meditative state is often referred to as the 'alpha state', the designated term for the brainwave patterns produced by meditation. This state also has a much wider effect on the physiological make-up of the person.

The alpha state is also reached during sleep - when totally relaxed, or even when daydreaming. However, as there are often different levels to one's sleep patterns, the electrical energies produced by the brain also vary, and move from alpha to theta and to delta. Being fully awake and getting on with life's daily chores is performed while the brain is in the beta state, in which numerous different feelings are experienced depending entirely on how the day is going for us.

The positive transformation of one's life must first of all begin with the certain knowledge that you do possess the power to transform it. Such a transformation involves the process of burning out the negative images of wrong thinking and the creation of new and more positive images, giving them enough energy to sustain them.

The cultivation of a much healthier and more vibrant aura may be achieved through the mental process of right thinking. In fact, I referred to it earlier as auric sculpturing - the mental process of creating a new personal atmosphere. The image-making faculty of the brain is an incredibly powerful tool, which can be used to create a new and more dynamic positive personality. Although the following exercise takes some time to grasp, once it is fully mastered there are many benefits.

FOCUSING THE MIND VISUALISATION EXERCISE
Phase One
Try to relax totally, either sitting in a comfortable chair or lying on the bed. Close your eyes and 'see' your life as it presently is, full of worries, problems and anxieties, allowing yourself for a few moments to relive each of these negative mental states. Allow your mind to go over all the things that present a problem for you and create a grey balloon around each one. Continue the process until you have a clear picture in your imagination of yourself clutching the strings attached to the grey balloons. In your mind, see yourself in control of the balloons and then, when you are quite ready, release them with a smile.

As the balloons float off into the air, again use the power of your imagination and will them to return to you and once again take hold of the strings. Hold onto the balloons for a moment, reaffirming what is contained within each of them and then, using your imagination once again, check that each balloon still represents each of your problems. Then release the balloons again and watch them float off into the air. Allow them to move a little further away than before and then draw them back towards you again and reach out and take hold of the strings.

Continue this process for as long as it takes for you to feel comfortable with the exercise.

When you feel confident that you fully understand the object of the exercise and have begun to feel as though your problems are mentally under control, you can consider the next phase. Although the cause of your worry and despair is objective, the actual feelings themselves are created subjectively. It is therefore at a subliminal level that the work must take place.

Phase Two
Seeing the balloons very clearly in your imagination, reach out and burst them, one by one, allowing a moment to elapse between each impact. Be mindful of the fact that with each destroyed balloon goes your worry and despair. Sit for a few moments relaxing before considering the next phase.

I am not suggesting for one moment that this exercise of the imagination will magically eradicate your financial difficulties, health problems, or any other seemingly insurmountable obstacle that you may be encountering in your everyday life, nor am I suggesting that you ignore these problems completely. On the contrary, life is difficult enough without adding complications. However, by learning to master the immense powers of your imagination, you may exert more positive control over your life, enabling you to become the master. Such a dramatic transformation of self has a much wider effect, not only on your mental state but also on your physical and spiritual ones.

Phase Three

Allow your body to relax even more by breathing slowly and deeply, taking even breaths. Clear your mind completely, without making it a labour. Feel yourself sinking almost into a state of sleep, totally relaxed and overwhelmed with a beautiful sense of peace and calm. When you feel relaxed enough, allow your imagination to light up the screen in your mind.

Now begin to focus totally on those things that you desire, such as prosperity, health, happiness and peace of mind, and place each in order of importance to you. Create a brightly lit white balloon around each desire, and once again take hold of their strings. Allow your imagination to focus on each balloon and what that balloon represents.

See the balloons glowing in your imagination, gleaming brightly as they float in front of you. Look into each of the balloons and see the things you desire written very clearly in brightly glowing words. Then, as you did with the grey balloons, release them, allowing them to float upwards.

Watch the balloons move away from you and then, using the strength and powers of your imagination as before, watch them being slowly drawn back towards you. When the balloons are close enough, reach out, take hold of the strings and pull them nearer to you. Once again, check the contents of each balloon, and make them glow even more brightly.

Repeat the process over and over again until you feel confident that you have them all under your control. (Should you still be unsure of the measure of your control over the balloons and what they represent, leave the exercise and come back to it another time.)

Once you fully comprehend the object of the exercise and you feel confident about your control over the balloons, consider all the balloons and the feelings, desires and emotions they represent, and create a word that collectively encapsulates them. This can be anything you like, from 'control' to 'power', so long as it is a word that you fully understand. Focus on it for as long as it takes to familiarise yourself completely with it. Remember that you have created this word and therefore understand the power behind it. Explore the word fully, occasionally allowing your thoughts to reconsider the things that the word represents for you.

When you have total confidence in the word and what is contained within it, allow your imagination to return to the white balloons. See them clearly in front of you and destroy them one by one, dissolving them completely from the screen in your imagination.

Phase Four

When you feel ready, move on to the next phase. Again relax your body as deeply as you possibly can, clearing all the residual images from your mind, and allow yourself to drift once again to the point of sleep. In fact, repeat to yourself, 'I will not sleep, I will only allow myself to be as totally relaxed as I possibly can', while breathing in and out slowly and deeply.

Once you have achieved a feeling of serenity, allow your imagination to light up the screen in your mind again. Place your chosen word on the screen so that you can see it clearly. You are now going to convert that word into three separate finger positions which, when executed, will enable you instantly to release the inherent forces of your original desires.

First of all, familiarise yourself with the three separate movements, which represent three different levels of achievement:

Movement One

Place your index finger of either hand between your brows for a

83

brief moment. This movement will enable you to be assertive, confident and able to cope in any difficult situation. In fact, the movement of your index finger to the space between your brows increases your capacity to concentrate and to project your personal magnetism, thereby affording you the confidence you require when under pressure. Interviews, starting a new career, exams, beginning new ventures, going it alone in business, using your powers of observation, solving problems, thinking things through - in other words, anything that requires you to be alert and attentive - may be achieved with the simple movement of the index finger to the brow.

The finger movement has a subliminal psychological effect   on the brow chakra - Ajna - and will precipitate all the required qualities that have been created in the mental exercise.

Movement Two

Touch the tip of your nose briefly with the middle finger of your right hand to release your deeper magnetic powers, so enabling you to overcome financial problems and gain a greater and more positive control over your financial life. By touching the tip of your nose you can overcome loneliness and feelings of insecurity, increasing your powers to attract new friends, good health, wealth, and a greater sense of adventure. This finger position also helps you to become more patient, astute and meticulous, and will also release those inner magnetic powers, encouraging the 'Midas touch' in all that you do.

Once this technique has been fully mastered, this finger position helps to activate the channels of energy between the throat chakra - Vishudda - and brow chakra - Ajna - affording you a greater and more powerful force of attraction.

The only cautionary note I would sound here is that this finger position must not be used for selfish means or to hurt others, because this may cause the opposite effect to be experienced, reintroducing all the original negative situations and emotions with a force far greater than before.

Movement Three

Touch your throat briefly with the little finger of your right hand to release a surge of psychic power, allowing you to see things much more clearly.

This finger movement will make you more intuitive, and will also aid the self-healing process for those recovering from illness. It will precipitate creative and psychic abilities, making them stronger and more efficient. It also helps to encourage general awareness, making you more receptive to other people's thoughts and feelings.

This finger position releases the inherent powers of the throat chakra - Vishudda - and affects your whole awareness and perception of objects, situations and people. It can also be of assistance when you are struggling to diet.

These three finger positions themselves will have no effect at all if the accompanying visualisation exercise has not been followed and practised regularly. To enable them to really work for you a programme has to be created first.

It is a good idea to make a list of all the things you would like to change in your life and all the things you want to achieve before attempting the exercise.

Although the exercise in creative visualisation is important in making the finger positions work for you, try not to make it too complicated for yourself. For instance, keep the number of balloons in the exercise to a minimum; you may even allow each balloon to contain more than one thing.

You will also find it of value to the outcome and effectiveness of the finger positions if you associate each balloon with one of them. For example, one or two balloons may contain a desire for wealth and happiness, in which case focus on these for a few moments and then apply the finger to the corresponding position, thereby setting the programme in motion.

It may be the case that you find it easier to modify the exercise in some way in order to suit your own grasp and understanding of it. This will not adversely affect the results provided that the creative imagery exercise has been practised until the programme has been fully established in your mind. Remember, it does take time and practice to make the exercise work for you, but you can rest assured that your perseverance and determination will produce positive rewards.

Even when the technique has been fully mastered it is advisable to practise it as regularly as possible in order to reintroduce the imagery into the subconscious and to revitalise it with more power. It may also be that you want to reprogramme the exercise occasionally, having achieved your previous aims. I would certainly suggest that you do this, as your abilities will benefit from an occasional 'clear out', just as though you were discarding an old and worn videotape and replacing it with a new and much clearer one.

The aura in fact becomes much stronger and more vibrant when the mind is used to its highest potential, and exercises such as those just given encourage a more positive outlook and personality. However, if you are really serious about the cultivation of your aura, I cannot stress too much the importance of your fullest co-operation when practising the visualisation techniques in the programme. To reiterate what I have said early, my approach to the cultivation of the senses is purely holistic, and the exercises in the book consider the whole person - body, mind and soul.

CHAPTER SEVENTEEN
ENCOURAGING THE
IMAGE-MAKING FACULTY

It is perhaps only over the last 15 years or so that science has made any real effort to comprehend the concept of time, to the extent that one notable scientist has had to rethink his theories about time and the possibility of travelling through it.

Time, in fact, is one of those great mysteries that man has always found quite difficult to comprehend, although it has always held a great fascination for the writers of science fiction who have exploited the subject to the full, exciting and catching the imagination of millions of readers with stories of time travel and time exploration.

In fact, to enable man to live with time, he has arbitrarily divided it into a past, a present and a future. He restricts himself to the confines of the past and the present, thinking the future to be beyond the range of his vision. He compartmentalises the events that he has already experienced into the section of his memory labelled 'the past', and at times he apparently has great difficulty in dealing with the present until that, too, is ready to be placed in the section labelled 'the past'.

Man has no difficulty in recalling the past to the present, but he tends to perceive the future rather like a blind man wandering alone in some strange, mysterious land, almost as though he has an inherent dread of it.

Space, however, appears to present a far smaller problem to man. This, at least, seems to be more obvious to him, in as much as he is able to move more freely in space than he can in time. He can move forwards, backwards and sideways in space, and now he has learned to move outwards and upwards, thus conquering the limitations imposed on his predecessors, by designing and building flying machines and spacecrafts.

It would thus appear that science is only just beginning to bring into reality the images, impressions and dreams of the science fiction writers of the last 60 years or more. Could it therefore be that the mind is truly the common denominator? Could each one of us be linked to the other, and could all in some way be connected to a universal reservoir, in which the past, the present and the future are experienced as one? Is it not a fact that the astronaut makes a mockery of time when he perceives the Earth from a great height, with the nights, days and time differences of all the countries in the world visibly manifested together, all at the same time?

We are most certainly limited, in more ways than one, by our brains and the way in which they have evolved. The arrangement of a cerebral lobe, and the addition of a fine network of nerves to those that form our consciousness, would no doubt be all that is needed to make the future unfold itself before us, with the selfsame clarity and majestic amplitude as that with which the past is displayed on the horizons of our memory.

Perhaps in the future man will have mastered the art of manipulating time and travelling through it. If this were true, and the future has already happened, why has no one travelled back to inform us of what they know? Perhaps they have, and perhaps the past to which future man has travelled is not the present that we know and are experiencing at this moment.

Perhaps the universe itself is not what it appears to our ephemeral minds. It is certainly multidimensional by its very nature, with world existing within world, each rising in a gradually ascending vibratory scale to the very highest realms in the cosmos.

Man, it would appear, is used to mentally looking in one direction, and that is to the past. He regards the future as being out of bounds, and is probably afraid of what he might see.

The future has always held a great fascination for man - a curious and at times naïve fascination that was often exploited by the ancient seers and visionaries whom man would consult for information about his future. Needless to say, not all seers in ancient times were genuine. However, those who were had long since discovered a way of gaining access into that mysterious land

88

of the future, even though some of the strange and weird methods of divination used by them in doing so would no doubt be ridiculed or frowned on today. Some seers, however, needed nothing at all to help them to see into the future, and would often appear to stare vacantly into space in order to glean the information they required.

Once your psychic ability has shown signs of manifesting, the art of 'staring' can be perfected with practice, and the ability to perceive the future developed in time.

It is possible that your psychic skill presently manifests as no more than strong intuitive feelings, and that you neither 'see' nor 'hear' anything that could be regarded as a psychic experience. You may also still have a lot of self-doubt regarding the possibility of your being psychic, and you may still discount any strong, extraordinary feelings that you experience, putting them down to intuition. However, you must understand that intuitive abilities manifest through the same faculties as do psychic abilities, and they are often all that remains in most people of the primitive mechanism of the survival faculty.

The devout sceptic denies the existence of psychic abilities, but will readily accept the existence of intuition simply because it is traditionally regarded as quite credible by society, whilst psychic abilities are not.

It would be incredibly difficult to describe the taste of sugar to someone who has never tasted it, or to describe colour to a person who has been visually handicapped from birth. In the same way, it is equally difficult to describe exactly what it is like being psychic to a person who has never experienced it.

We have all experienced the natural phenomenon of daydreaming - staring blankly into space as nebulous pictures pass, sometimes nostalgically, across our consciousness. But, while daydreaming, how many times have pictures or images that you did not recognise floated across your mind? The natural reaction to these is to discount them and put them down to pure imagination.

The faculty responsible for the psychic ability of 'clairvoyance' manifests in various unexpected ways. The images produced through the process of daydreaming also manifest from that same faculty, and can be developed and cultivated with the use of the same techniques. But what use would there be in developing the ability to daydream merely to recall pictures of one's past? The cultivation of the image-making faculty encourages the development of the creative senses, a prerequisite for the development of 'clairvoyance'.

DEVELOPING YOUR ABILITY TO DAYDREAM INTO THE FUTURE

I have used the term 'daydream' as an example in order to help you understand exactly how most clairvoyance impressions appear. They can often be quite nebulous, even when the ability has been developed into a fine art. Even when one has undergone extensive training and possesses an extremely accurate psychic ability, demonstrations of such powers must always be looked on as purely experimental, because the results of such demonstrations are rarely consistent. However, practice does make it as perfect as it can be.

Gazing - Exercise One

* Take a piece of matt black cardboard, measuring approximately 2ft (60cm) square, and paint a white dot in the very centre. Then take a piece of white cardboard of the same size, and in the centre paint a black dot.
* Prop up both cards in front of you, at a distance of approximately 3ft (90cm) away, with the dots facing you and as near to eye level as possible.
* Spend a few moments relaxing with your eyes closed, and attempt to make your mind as quiet as possible. You can encourage this process with some slow, rhythmic breathing. Breathe slowly and deeply, keeping your eyes closed and allowing your stomach to rise as you breathe in, and to fall as you breathe out. Continue this for a few minutes until you are relaxed and your mind is totally quiet.
* Once you are perfectly relaxed, open your eyes and slowly move your gaze to the white dot in the centre of the black card. Focus

your gaze on this dot, resisting the temptation to blink or to move your eyes away even for a moment, as this will defeat the object of the exercise. (Should you find it impossible to gaze any longer without blinking, then blink, but do not move your eyes away from the central dot even for a split second.)

* When you can hold your gaze no longer, slowly close your eyes and place your hands over them, applying a little pressure to the eyeballs with the palms of your hands. Wait for the after-image to appear slowly in your mind's eye.

* Watch the image float around your consciousness for a few moments, breathing in and out slowly and deeply and willing the image to become brighter and more clearly defined every time you breathe in. Retain the image in your mind's eye for a few moments, and then turn your attention to the white card.

* Open your eyes and allow your gaze to focus on the black dot in the centre of the white card, and then repeat the staring process. As you gaze at the black dot, you will notice how the previous after-image of the black card appears to be superimposed over the white card, but continue to gaze at the black dot, resisting any distraction you may feel from this after-image.

* When you can no longer hold your gaze, slowly close your eyes and watch the new after-image being introduced into your consciousness.

* Continue this exercise for a maximum of 15 to 20 minutes, alternating the cards as you repeat the process.

Practise this exercise at least three times a week, more if possible. This particular technique has the effect of stimulating the visual response mechanism of the brain, eventually precipitating the clairvoyant ability. I must stress, however, that when I use the word 'clairvoyance' I am using it in the traditional way, meaning 'clear-seeing', to see into the future.

The person who has no great difficulty in visualising images and who can create pictures in the mind's eye with ease has a far greater chance of developing the ability of clairvoyance than does someone who struggles to visualise. The process of clairvoyance involves the image-making faculty of the brain. Artists, or anyone who works on a creative level, quite often possess potential psychic abilities, and they probably experience these in their work from time to time without even realising it.

Gazing - Exercise Two

In order to obtain the maximum results this exercise requires a partner and the use of a cassette or DVD recorder to record the whole experiment.

* Using the black card only (see previous exercise), seat yourself in front of the propped-up card and ask your partner to sit behind it.
* Ask your partner to project a mental picture (the subject matter can be anything at all, whether simple or complex) to you through the black part of the card, while you focus your gaze on the white dot.
* Whilst gazing at the white dot you should allow your mind to remain passively empty and make no attempt to receive the picture your partner is sending.
* When you can no longer gaze at the dot, close your eyes and place the palms of your hands over them, watching the after-image appear very slowly in your mind's eye. It is approximately at this point that your partner's mental impression should gradually become visible to you.
* At first nothing may happen, but if you persevere with the experiment you should begin to receive vague impressions of fragmented images. Of course, you may not see anything very clearly and may just be overwhelmed with vague sensations. Whatever it is that you experience, you must voice it immediately. This often makes any impressions received grow stronger and much clearer.
* If at first you are not successful, ask your partner to transmit another picture. In my experience the composition of the picture is not important. It can be anything from a simple image to an extremely complex pattern. If the exercise is going to work, it will work just as well with an intricate design as it will with a single, solitary line.

Once you have mastered the technique, and developed a rapport with your partner, a telepathic relationship will become apparent in the results that you obtain.

By practising this sort of exercise, you will eventually discover your own technique and way of achieving the desired results.

Most people who show even the slightest interest in psychic matters often do so because of an experience that they themselves have had at some time or another, which has left them with the feeling that there is more to be developed. When cornered, even the most ardent cynic will admit that he or she has had an unusual psychic experience at some time.

The most common experiences that people have are knowing of someone's death long before the news arrives, or knowing the phone is going to ring before it does, and perhaps even knowing who the caller will be. These kinds of experiences (precognitive) transcend the bounds of coincidence, particularly as they usually happen more than once.

I have often heard it said of psychics that they possess overactive imaginations or that they are too sensitive. These accusations are correct on both counts. A strong, active imagination appears to be a prerequisite for the development of psychic abilities, and the stronger the abilities the more sensitive the psychic. I would hope that with the help of the exercises in this book you will be able to control your sensitivity, and learn how to channel it in a positive way. To reiterate an extremely important point: all psychic skills manifest through the medium of the aura, and the stronger and more consistent the aura, the more efficient your psychic skills will be.

Furthermore, in order to develop your psychic skills further, you must allow your imagination to work for you. To suppress it in any way will merely inhibit any latent psychic tendencies. You must, therefore, give your imagination its freedom and allow your creative faculties to be active.

USING THE IMAGINATION TO CULTIVATE YOUR PSYCHIC SKILLS

In my experience I have found that there is a close connection between the image-making faculty of the brain and the faculties responsible for the skill of clairvoyance. Should you not have the ability to visualise and create images in your mind, then I am afraid you will never cultivate the art of clairvoyance. However, the image-making faculty can be exercised just like any other faculty, and although the exercises used solely for this purpose are extremely simple, they do work.

The following exercise involves the imagination and a little guesswork.

Exercise for Improving the Image-Making Faculty
For this experiment you will need a partner again, and an empty box with a lid.
* Close your eyes and sit quietly.
* Ask your partner, out of view, to place a small mystery object of their choice inside the box and close the lid.
* Visualise the box surrounded by a very bright white light, and imagine yourself breathing the bright light deep into your lungs and into the solar plexus.
* Continue to focus all your attention on the image of the box in your mind, and look on the box as a conscious entity, full of life, to whom you can speak and which will also listen. To animate the box in your mind you might even find it helpful to make it into a sort of cartoon character with features, such as eyes, a mouth and legs, etc.
* Ask the box to reveal its contents to you and wait for the answer. No matter how ridiculous the answer seems, repeat it to your partner, who should then tell you immediately whether or not you are correct.
* Limit yourself to six attempts at discovering the box's contents. If you have not been successful by then, ask your friend to exchange the hidden item for another.
* If you have difficulty in picturing the box as an animated cartoon figure with whom you can converse, focus your attention on the image of the box in your mind and slowly rotate it in your mind's eye, looking at it from every conceivable angle. Then try to imagine your way into the box and take a look at the contents.

94

Allow your imagination as much freedom as possible, regardless of how silly you think it is.

* Alternatively, imagine yourself picking up the box to ascertain its weight. Then, whilst holding it mentally in your hands, see yourself lifting the lid and peering inside.

* You should tell your partner the first thing you see in your mind's eye. Should you be correct, repeat the experiment with another article straight away.

The object of the exercise is to encourage the imagination to create images. Do not dismiss the exercise because it seems silly and therefore will not work. It is purely an exercise in imagination, and it helps to strengthen the image-making faculty in much the same way that you can exercise the body in the gym to increase its strength and power.

It is important that you do not question how you obtained successful results in the exercise. Do not add doubt by saying it was achieved solely by guesswork. How you do it is not important. If you achieve a success rate of six or more out of ten, apparently by guessing, then that is the way it will work for you. Accurate information is often obtained by psychics who appear to guess. Once a psychic ability develops, the way in which it works for you should not be questioned, so long as it is a reliable method that produces positive results.

Precognitive skills - glimpses of the future, which I have already briefly touched on, are more common than one might imagine. They often display themselves as overwhelming feelings of apprehension - perhaps a strong, intuitive feeling, regarding a stranger, or an approaching situation. Sometimes we are 'impressed' to act on impulse, or we perhaps feel pleasurable anticipation about an approaching opportunity, or about a situation that, to everyone else, appears quite depressing.

These strong feelings may only be experienced occasionally, and they often come without any preliminary warning. Nonetheless, they are very real to the person who experiences them and should therefore be accepted as one of probably many psychic abilities that they possess.

CHAPTER EIGHTEEN
LOOKING FORWARD
THROUGH TIME

Even though you may now possess a fairly strong and reliable psychic ability, you may still not yet have developed, or mastered, the art of looking forward into the future. Until you have actually experienced this phenomenon you will not know exactly what to look for. You may have imposed limitations on yourself by only experimenting with those methods whose results can be immediately confirmed.

Before attempting to develop the ability to look into the future, you must try to understand that by controlling the mind, instead of allowing the mind to control you, you can influence the dynamic forces of the future.

In theory, precognition and prophetic vision are the same, but there is one small difference: precognition is mostly involuntary, and the gift of prophecy, although it can happen spontaneously, can be controlled.

Before any attempt is made to develop the ability to prophesy the future, you should first have some understanding of the principles underlying the mechanics of awareness. Human awareness manifests at four different levels, and one's consciousness has an experience at all of these levels at some time or another, often without your even realising it.

For instance, you may be driving home from work through the rush-hour traffic, mentally going over what you need to do later on, and completely oblivious to your driving. You suddenly become aware that you have parked your car in your driveway, and you have done so with no recollection of the journey you have just made.

It would almost seem as though, within us all, there is an 'automatic pilot' which takes over when we are out of control. The same can be said for when we are faced with an arduous task for the first time, one that demands a great deal of concentration. While our attention is focused entirely on the job at hand we are completely oblivious to all else around us, and totally unaware of any sound or distraction. However, once the task has been mastered it can be brought under the control of our 'automatic pilot' and, if necessary, be carried out with little or no concentration.

The first and lowest level of human awareness is one that we all experience, all the time. Through this level we gain our knowledge of the world in which we live. The second level of awareness is also shared by everyone, but usually only in times of stress, anxiety, or activation of the survival reflex - that is, when we are under threat of danger.

However, the examples I have given above are in the extreme. In actuality, this second level of awareness is also the aspect of consciousness in which we are capable of achieving extraordinary things. It is subdivided into two aspects: the first takes control of our anxieties and the need to survive, and the second appears to elevate our consciousness into and through the third level of awareness, so bringing about a greater realisation of the impulses received from the fourth level of awareness, which is that of spirit.

We are limited by terminology in our definitions of these levels of awareness, so I will refer to them as physical awareness, instinctive awareness, intellectual awareness, and spiritual awareness.

Intellectual awareness represents the thinker in man. It is the level at which he enquires and analyses. It represents the 'I' consciousness, through which man seeks knowledge and expression. Depending on the degree of consciousness he has of the fourth level (that of spiritual awareness), the intellectual level of awareness can be extremely cold, arrogant, self-opinionated and cynical. At its more positive, the intellectual level of awareness brings man ideas and makes him an innovator. Through this level the higher spiritual or real self can express its feelings, bringing into man's consciousness spiritual revelations, light and inspiration.

97

Through the fourth level, spiritual awareness, man experiences divine inspiration and that closeness to God in that place of light. Having experienced a level of spiritual awareness, man realises that words alone will not in any way represent what he has discovered. His tongue appears ineffectual, almost as though some secret command has been given, hushing him to silence.

The spiritual level of awareness does not in any way overpower the third level of intellectual awareness, it simply transcends it, passing down to it the experiences acquired in it's own level of the spiritual mind. These are yet again explored and then processed at the intellectual level of awareness, whereon man analyses and reasons about them.

Before attempting to use psychic powers to prophesy the future, you need first of all to experience the various levels of awareness at which they are acquired, to enable the route of entry to be reliably accessible. In this way results can be successfully achieved each time.

EXERCISE IN AWARENESS

This exercise has been designed to enable you to experience varying degrees of emotional, mental and spiritual awareness. It is often productive of suppressed emotions, by making you aware of old and deeply buried fears, anxieties and sorrows. It is more an exercise in self-awareness than of meditation, and often promotes a greater realisation of the soul and its independence of the body.

To achieve the desired results, the exercise must be practised with total dedication. Allow it to create for you a sanctuary, or inner sanctum, into which you can retreat when seeking peace and serenity. So long as you follow the visualisation procedure as I have given it, nothing else is required of you. The object of the exercise is to allow it to produce symbols, pictures and other metaphors that you should interpret when the meditation is concluded.

* Find a comfortable chair and relax for a few moments with your eyes closed. Make your mind as quiet as you possibly can, in the usual way of breathing slowly and deeply for a few moments.

* Focus your thoughts totally on yourself, and silently say to yourself, 'My body is not me. I merely reside in it, and may leave it at any time I wish, but I must return to it when the exercise is concluded.'
* Repeat this three or four times, fixing it firmly in your mind, and then begin the visualisation:

Imagine yourself standing on the worn stone steps of a beautiful old monastery. Look down at the steps and notice the texture and colour of the stone, and the uneven cracks running through them. The ornately carved oak doors of the monastery slowly open, and as you look up you see the aged, frail figure of a monk standing in the doorway. Your eyes take in the heavy brown cloth of his habit and the pale skin of his elderly, wrinkled face. He smiles at you and raises his hand in a welcoming gesture.

Follow the monk as he turns and walks through the doorway into the monastery. As the doors slowly close behind you they bring a veil of stillness down around you, and you become aware of the quiet, calm atmosphere of the monastery. Follow the old man as he makes his way slowly down a shadowy passageway, lit only by flickering lamps strategically positioned on the stone walls on either side of you. Dark shadows reach across the floor in front of you. Your heart quickens in anticipation as you hasten to keep up with the old monk, whose shuffling footsteps echo off the walls. You emerge into a huge, round, brightly lit hall. The high, domed, stained-glass ceiling allows a cascade of colour to pool down on the marble, mosaic floor, which appears to glisten and sparkle as if it, too, is made of glass. As you look around you notice that the walls of the hall appear translucent. They shimmer like mother-of-pearl. You notice several monks moving contemplatively around you, chanting to an accompaniment of chimes. For a moment you remain still, listening to the chanting.

Smiling, your elderly guide gestures towards a doorway on the other side of the hall. You obediently walk across the cool marble floor towards it. By the time you reach the door it is already open. Through the doorway you can see a narrow wooden staircase leading upwards. Move towards it, and stand for a moment at the foot of the stairs. Watch the sunlight stream in through a high window on the landing above you, throwing shards of bright light across the floor and walls. In the distance you can still hear the rhythmic chanting of the monks.

Slowly begin to ascend the stairs, one step at a time, feeling a rush of excitement as you climb higher and higher. Follow the staircase as it turns to the left. A few more steps and you find yourself standing alone on the first landing, gazing curiously down the long, narrow passageway in front of you. There is a sweet fragrance in the air, and a sense of peace and well-being overwhelms you. You become aware of an extremely strong, familiar feeling of having been here before.

As you look along the passageway you notice three doors on the left-hand side and two doors on the right. At the very end of the passage, facing you, there is one door. Pause for a few moments before moving to the door of your choice.

Before choosing a door it is important to realise that at this level you are given the opportunity to deal with all those negative, self-destructive thoughts and emotions. You are now at the second level, or what I have called 'instinctive awareness', and it is important that, on entering the room of your choice, you either immediately rearrange it to your liking, or simply remove an item of furniture, or anything else you find unpleasant, from the room. Before you leave the room you must feel comfortable with it.

Now enter the room of your choice and close the door gently behind you. Have a good look around. Observe the walls, the windows, the furniture, and the rugs on the floor. Sit down on a chair for a few moments, imbibing the atmosphere. Then change anything you do not feel comfortable with.

Now you must leave. Move towards the door. Pause for a moment to have a last look around the room. Open the door and move into the corridor, closing the door behind you as you leave. Before moving away from the room, mentally prepare yourself for the next level - that of 'intellectual awareness'. This is the level at which ideas will come to you. You will feel strongly inspired at that level, and may even decide that you do not wish to go any further. Should this be the case, do not in any way question the apprehension you feel; simply leave, and return to the ground floor, the first level.

Now continue along the corridor to the staircase at the end. Climb the stairs very slowly, allowing your hand to brush against the cool stone wall. It feels solid and secure beneath your fingers. Once again, the feeling of anticipation rushes through you. Within moments you reach the next level.

At the top of the stairs you move directly into a small study. There are shelves on shelves of books around the walls, and a desk on which you notice a writing quill resting in an inkwell. There is a blank piece of parchment lying next to it. A fire is burning brightly in a fireplace, which is surrounded by a beautifully designed mantel. You can feel the heat from the fire as the flames blaze up the chimney. Sit in the armchair in front of the fire for a few moments, allowing the peace and serenity of the study to wash over you. At the same time reflect on your visit to the monastery, and your reason for coming.

This level particularly is very often productive of symbols, ideas and overwhelming feelings. Make your mind completely open to them.

Rise from the chair and move over to the desk. Mentally take the quill firmly in your hand and scribble on the parchment the first word that comes to mind. Have a good look around the room. Feel contemplative, mentally alert, and completely open to the impulses from the next level - that of 'spiritual awareness'. Make a mental note of what you have written on the parchment, and move away from the desk.

Leave the study and walk back towards the head of the staircase. Your eyes search for the way up to the next level, but there do not appear to be any stairs. Stand for a few moments contemplating the way forward.

You suddenly realise that the only access route to the fourth level is through your own imagination.

Imagine yourself standing and holding out your arms, whilst staring upwards. Imagine an intense white light above you, as if shining through the ceiling. Allow that bright light to descend slowly and envelop you. Feel the light all around you, interpenetrating every cell of your body. You feel totally disorientated and lose all sense of your surroundings. Almost at once you feel the bright light gradually fading into nothingness, and you find yourself standing in a beautifully lit sanctuary, in the centre of which there is a comfortable armchair. Sit down in the chair and enjoy the peace, quiet and solitude. Feel totally at peace in that sanctuary, allowing your imagination to create whatever it wishes. Be aware of every aspect of your surroundings and of the sweet fragrance wafting over you in the stillness. Remain there for as long as you wish. It may be that you will lose all sense of time, for time does not exist at the fourth level, where all answers lie.

When you are ready to leave, simply allow the quiet sanctuary to fade slowly from your consciousness. Find yourself standing at the top of the stairs on the third level.

Move slowly down the stairs, taking in your surroundings as you descend, eventually reaching the second level. Without pausing, continue to move down the stairs to the ground floor and the first level. Pass through the small door into the spacious round room with the domed ceiling and the mosaic floor. There you are greeted by the elderly monk. This time, pay particular attention to his aged, lined face. Notice his eyes, which are warm and friendly. Feel secure and safe with him, for next time you must greet him as an old friend.

Follow the old man across the mosaic floor, this time paying attention to the intricate detail in the design of the patterns on the floor. Follow him back along the shadowy passageway until you reach the monastery doors. Open them, and move outside into the cool, fresh breeze that gently brushes your hair. Turn and bid your guide farewell. Mentally ask him if you may return. He nods his answer with a warm smile and then closes the doors.

* Breathe very slowly and deeply a few times, and dissolve the whole exercise completely from your mind. Relax for a few moments in your chair.

Although quite long, this has been an exercise in awareness and imagination, and is one that must be used as often as possible in order to obtain the best results. You will find whatever you desire to know of the future at the fourth level. However, it will take time and patience before you achieve the desired results. Once the energies have been created in the exercise, your prophetic intuition will begin to produce glimpses of anything you wish to know. As I have already explained, the answers will most probably come in the form of symbols, metaphors and abstract pictures.

Once you have developed an affinity with the exercise, and you have come to understand it fully, you can begin to explore its possibilities in a more confident way. Having confidence in the exercise, and allowing yourself to become totally involved with it, is of primary importance. However, the most difficult result to accept and to deal with can often be the sudden rush of feelings that eventually surfaces from the bottom of the pool of emotion. Although the exercise appears to be quite simple, please do not underestimate it. It is an extremely effective exercise in psychology, and when practised properly it will have an incredible holistic effect on all aspects of the aura.

CHAPTER NINETEEN
TUNING THE AURA AND
YOUR KEY OF LIFE

THE EFFECTS OF MUSIC ON THE AURA

Recent scientific research into the effects of music on the human psyche has concluded that music is integrated into our biological make-up and that our genetic structure is actually encoded with music, making us what we are. In fact, even though we humans have taken millions of years to evolve into the sentient, self-aware beings we are today, music has always been there, tightly woven into virtually every culture across the planet.

Not only does music have a profound effect on the brain, it also has a significant 'washing' effect on the bioluminescence of the aura, thus making it more stabilised and together. Music produces theta brainwaves similar to those in deep relaxation and stage one of sleep. For many people music can be just as effective as and more therapeutic than the process of meditation. It has an extremely calming effect on the brain and central nervous system and absorbs our attention, distracting our thoughts completely away from worries and anxieties. Music consistently inputs the brain with mental stimuli, encouraging the sensory receptors to close down for a while and thus allowing the body to relax.

Music encourages pleasurable memories to surface and, although there is no definite scientific evidence for it, music may even evoke memories within the DNA of past life experiences.

Of course, all music is different; some we like and some we don't like. Some music stimulates the brain and stirs the body into activity, whilst other more serenely composed music has the effect of calming and quietening the mind and encouraging sleep. Therefore, the correct music has to be chosen in order to affect the aura and make it more stabilised and smooth. In fact, music produces long-term effects on the bioluminescence of the aura, and studies have shown that music can heal a broken or fragmented aura and even encourage a more consistent flow of energy and colour to the overall bioluminescence.

AURIC TUNING

If you perceive the whole human form as a sequence of musical sounds, then you may be able to appreciate the concept of 'auric tuning', and then see that the body itself is rather like a musical instrument and will occasionally go completely out of tune. The following chapter will explore the 'personal key' concept and analyse how we can retune our bodies to promote perfect harmony.

Some people have the unusual skill of being able to 'listen' to their own body and to know exactly when it is even slightly off key. These people are quite fortunate and nearly always enjoy good health. The individual particles that comprise the whole body mass collectively culminate into a sound, in fact a musical tone. This one individual tone is the combined sound of various notes created at different points and levels in the body. Should one of these notes be slightly off key, then the overall sound will appear slightly out of tune, just like listening to someone who is tone deaf singing one of your favourite songs. When the body is perfectly in tune, it has a resonance and is in perfect harmony with everything and everyone else. This means that the body, mind and spirit are balanced too and that the overall equilibrium is perfectly synchronised.

We have previously discussed the major chakras and their function as transformer-like units, modifying the volume and intensity of inflowing energy, and now we need to turn our attention to the musical value of each of the seven major chakras. Each chakra emits a note, and each note vibrates to a particular colour, from the lowest on the visible spectrum (red) to the highest (violet/purple):

Chakra	Note	Colour
1st (base)	C	Red
2nd (splenic)	D	Orange
3rd (solar plexus)	E	Yellow
4th (heart)	F	Green
5th (throat)	G	Blue
6th (brow)	A	Indigo
7th (crown)	B	Violet/purple

Although the function of the chakra system is potentially the same in everybody, in most people one particular chakra tends to predominate. The sound of this chakra is generally an indication as to the person's 'key of life', and as a consequence of stress, worry, poor diet and general wrong living its sound may sharpen or flatten. This is not too detrimental to an individual's overall balance if the chakra's key only sharpens or flattens a semitone, but when it is subjected to 'overtuning' as a result of living life in the fast lane, so to speak, the chakra's pitch moves a full tone and so changes key completely. When this change of key takes place it becomes difficult to normalise the chakra again. This usually causes the individual to become highly stressed and oversensitive.

The most sensitive and spiritual individuals are those who live in the third chakra around the solar plexus and the seventh chakra on the crown of the head. In music the sounds of these chakras do not, technically speaking, have sharps. However, the third chakra resonates to the note of E, which when it sharpens becomes F, and the seventh chakra resonates to the note of B, which when it sharpens becomes C. Highly spiritually developed individuals, such as those who devote their lives to prayer and meditation, usually live out their lives in Sahasrara, the crown chakra, and the resonating sound of B. Although crown chakra people do not normally live in the real world, they are usually together and well balanced, and so their other chakras are usually tuned and well aligned.

Although aligning and tuning the chakras will not solve all the problems that may have turned your life upside down, the process will enable you to perceive things in a much more positive and philosophical way.

Remember, the seven major chakras function as transformer-like units, and so it is their job to control, modify and distribute all the inpouring energy. So, although the entire physical body emits an extremely powerful sound, it is the collective unit of the chakras that has the job of converting that signal into one particular sound. And so, first of all you must discover your 'key of life'.

FINDING YOUR KEY OF LIFE EXERCISE

There are various more complicated ways of determining your key of life, but I always find the most effective way is also the simplest. For this you will need to enlist the help of a friend, and you will also require a pendulum and a musical instrument, or preferably a full octave of tuning forks, as this method is far more efficient and never fails to produce positive results.

* Lie in a horizontal position, either on the floor or a bed, whichever is more convenient and comfortable for you.
* Your friend should make sure the musical instrument or tunings forks are within reach.
* First of all, to ascertain the polarity of each chakra, they should be dowsed in sequence (see Chapter 10), beginning with the base chakra. Once a clockwise or anticlockwise motion has been established, move to the next chakra, and so on.
* Once all the chakras have been successfully dowsed and their individual movements established, the process of determining your key of life can commence.
* The middle note of C should be played on the musical instrument or sounded on a tuning fork, and this note should be sustained whilst the pendulum is held steadily over the first (base) chakra to see if its motion has changed and any differences should be noted down.
* If using a tuning fork, this should be placed more or less on the position of the chakra and the pendulum held over it.
* The second chakra should then be dowsed whilst sounding the note of D, again noting any changes in the rotation of the pendulum.

* Now, sound the note of E whilst dowsing the third chakra. In fact, pay particular attention to this point, ensuring that the note of E is sustained for as long as possible.
* Then move the pendulum to the fourth chakra whilst sounding the note of F, which should be sustained for a few moments.
* Sound the note of G whilst dowsing the fifth chakra, again ensuring that the note is sustained.
* Then, moving the pendulum carefully between the brows, sound the note of A, again sustaining it for a few moments. In fact, the polarity of this sixth chakra may fluctuate a little and so therefore may need to be dowsed again for confirmation.
* Although the seventh (crown) chakra is mostly dormant in the majority of people at this stage of evolution, it still must be considered when ascertaining one's key of life. Sound the note of B whilst dowsing the chakra in this area, ensuring that the note is sustained for a slightly longer period than for the others.

Now examine the results of this process to determine your key of life. The chakra displaying the most consistent movement is the one that should give you your overall key. However, once you have established that this is the predominant chakra, it should be checked further to ensure that the results have been accurate and not misread. The rotation of the chakra that has seemingly produced the most consistent activity should now be in the opposite direction to its initial one. Occasionally the chakra giving you your key of life may already rotate the opposite way to all the other chakras, but will appear to become more agitated once the appropriate note has been sounded.

Once you have found your key of life, balance may be maintained in the aura with the use of certain bija-mantras - special words designed to release the chakras' inherent properties. In fact, all individual chakras are synchronised with their own power word, and are also symbolically represented by a yantra - a geometric shape or design for the purpose of meditation.

In the following chapter we will explore how to maintain balance in the chakra system with the use of your key of life, and also how to encourage a stronger, more dynamic aura.

CHAPTER TWENTY
CHANTING YOUR WAY TO
A MORE FULFILLED LIFE

The use of bija-mantras and yantras is probably the safest and most effect way of precipitating the consciousness through the process of meditation. Even if you are one of those people who say "I can't meditate", everyone can chant and gaze. We chant all the time, whether it's just singing in the bath or cursing to ourselves about some stressful problem we are trying to deal with. Chanting makes us feel good by releasing tension and encouraging serenity and calmness. Although any word may be used as a mantra, in this particular process specific mantras are used. I have already explained that all chakras have a corresponding bija-mantra, and that a bija-mantra helps to activate and polarise the chakra to which it is synchronised. The word 'bija' simply means semen, centre or core. And so the bija-mantra infiltrates the essence and releases it into the consciousness. The method is quite easy and requires very little effort or, for that matter, concentration.

First of all, spend a little time studying the Sanskrit names for the chakras and their corresponding bija-mantras:

Chakra	Bija-mantra
Muladhara	Lam
Svadisthana	Vam
Manipura	Ram
Anahata	Yam
Vishudda	Ham
Ajna	Ksham
Sahasrara	Om (or Aum)

There are two different ways of using bija-mantras, one more specific than the other, although both are very effective in maintaining balance in the chakra system and the aura.

CHANTING - METHOD ONE

The first method is to focus on the chakra from which you have derived your key of life (see previous chapter) and then chant the associated word. The process of chanting is fairly straightforward and requires very little effort or mental involvement other than to watch your breathing.

* Spend a few moments relaxing the body and breathing rhythmically in the following way: inhale a complete breath and then slowly exhale, ensuring that the inhalations and exhalations are evenly spaced and that you do not strain them or make them a labour.

* When you feel quite relaxed and are ready to begin chanting, with your eyes closed slowly inhale a complete breath (making sure that your lungs are sufficiently full of air) and then, on the exhalation, sound your word as loudly as you possibly can, maintaining the depth and clarity of the chanting until the breath has been full expelled.

* Immediately draw in a deep and complete breath and repeat the process.

* Keep repeating the whole process of breathing in and chanting on the outbreath for about ten minutes at first. You can increase the length of time of your chanting once you become more accustomed to it.

* Should your word be 'Ksham', the 'K' is silent and so you should chant 'Sham', allowing the 'M' to resound until the breath fades into nothingness.

CHANTING - METHOD TWO

The second method of chanting I think is far more fun to do, and it is even more fun when practised in a group. Until you have memorised all the bija-mantras in sequential order, you will need to write them down.

* Sit with your chest, neck and head in as straight a line as possible, with your shoulders thrown slightly back and your hands resting

lightly on your lap.

* As before, spend a few minutes clearing the mind and relaxing, using unlaboured rhythmic breathing.

* When you are ready, inhale a complete breath and then on the exhalation begin chanting the words in quick succession, backwards and forwards, over and over again.

* Thus, the chanting should begin with LAM and conclude with OM, and then work back in reverse order to LAM, and so on.

* Should you be chanting in a group, make sure that your chanting is in unison and more or less in the same key.

* Once you have mastered the art of chanting and have got the rhythm exactly right, clap your hands with each intonation, chanting and clapping as loudly as you possibly can.

* When the chanting has been concluded, close your eyes and place your hands gently on your solar plexus. Feel your hands tingling and imagine the energy passing from your hands into your solar plexus and moving around your entire body.

* When you are ready, commence chanting again, repeating the whole process.

The chanting is quite invigorating and has a tendency to stimulate the energy levels in the practitioner's aura. Over a period of time it will heighten the awareness and encourage a more evenly balanced chakra system. In fact, the whole process has a sort of holistic effect on the entire subtle anatomy, stimulating the brain and making the bioluminescence clear and more intense.

Using yantras, or geometric shapes or designs, is perhaps a little more involved and, although the results can be quite amazing, the actual process of gazing at yantras does not suit everybody.

First of all, let us take a look at the actual yantras themselves:

Chakra	Yantra
Muladhara	Yellow square
Svadhisthana	Crescent moon
Manipura	Triangle (apex pointing down)
Anahata	Two interlaced triangles
Vishudda	Oval
Ajna	Circle

BIJI MANTRAS AND YANTRAS

CHAKRA	YANTRA	BIJA MANTRA
MULADHARA		'LAM'
SVADISTHANA		'VAM'
MANIPURA		'RAM'
ANAHATA		'YAM'
VISHUDDA		'HAM'
AJNA		'KSHAM'
SAHASRARA		'OM'

The yantra can either be used by itself or combined with the corresponding bija-mantra.

YANTRA GAZING METHOD

Used by itself, this process simply involves gazing at the centre of the yantra. First of all, though, you will need to paint the geometric shape on a cardboard square and prop it up in front of you at eye level and in subdued lighting.

* Sitting comfortably opposite the yantra, simply gaze at it without blinking or moving your eyes away even for a moment.
* When you can no longer gaze at the geometric shape, slowly close your eyes and allow the after-image to appear in your mind's eye.
* Hold the after-image in your mind's eye for as long as possible.
* When the after-image begins to fade and becomes fragmented, open your eyes, return your gaze to the yantra and repeat the whole process.
* When combining yantra gazing with bija-mantra chanting, simply gaze at the yantra as explained above, and when you close your eyes begin chanting the appropriate bija-mantra as explained in the first chanting method. Make certain that when you are chanting the sound is even and consistent, and that its sound is

carried to the full extent of the exhalation of your breath.

HARMONICS OF THE MIND

Regardless of what work you do, a strong and positive mind is a prerequisite for success, and without these attributes no form of success can be permanent. The way you think creates your character, and your thoughts are the materials with which you shape your life. Thoughts are living things; the stronger and more vibrant the thoughts, the longer those thoughts will persist in the space around you. In order to achieve fulfilment and a more successful life, the mind has to be synchronised with everything else around you. Correct attitude and right thinking are two attributes that are dictated by your circumstances, and should your circumstances not be conducive then it is difficult to develop these two important attributes. This is the proverbial catch-22 situation, rather like trying to create heaven using the materials of heaven itself.

Many, many years ago I found myself in very difficult circumstances, and I reached such a low ebb that I simply did not know where to turn. I eventually realised that I was looking to other people for a helping hand, but of course when you have nothing and find yourself in a desperate situation very few people are willing to give you the help that you need. I understood then that there was only one place to go, and that was within. In times of great need the only person you can truly rely on is yourself, and you will not let yourself down, that's for sure.

Of course, I am talking about meditation, the key to self-mastery, which will be discussed in the next chapter. When I talk about meditation I am not talking about simply closing your eyes and thinking nice, pleasant thoughts. I am referring to a system of mental control, in which you are able to focus on one thing to the exclusion of all else. Meditation is, in fact, the highest form of prayer. It is the means through which all great minds seek to attain fulfilment and attainment. Meditation is the mind's most powerful tool, and the energies created through meditation can cure a diseased body, promote serenity and calmness in the mind, and also facilitate success and opportunity.

113

CHAPTER TWENTY-ONE
MEDITATION - THE KEY
TO SELF-MASTERY

Throughout this book I have spoken about meditation in one form or another, and have stressed that what meditation technique suits one person may not necessarily suit another. Meditation is not just for a certain type of person, even though it still has 1960s connotations and is often associated with the hippy and flower power era. Nothing could be further from the truth, for meditation has been practised for thousands of years in the East, and in India today is even integrated into the educational curriculum, with the wise belief that meditation promotes calmness and encourages the ability to cope with stress.

When I speak of meditation, I am talking about a specific system of mental exercise in which discipline is exerted over one's mental processes with the sole object of cultivating a much greater awareness of the reality of the soul and its independence of the body, so encouraging the precipitation of consciousness. As this book is primarily about the magic of the aura, we will explore all the possibilities of meditation, and how it can work for you as a means of enhancing your awareness.

Although group meditation can be extremely effective when one is seeking to attain a higher level of consciousness, I believe that certain methods of meditation are simply not suitable for some people. For example, there are those who might find the practice of meditation within a group uncomfortable in one way or another. The effects of meditation certainly vary from person to person too, and often depend on the individual's personality, metabolism, mental and emotional processes, and their ability to concentrate. For example, some people may find it almost impossible to hold an abstract thought in their mind for a minute, let alone for ten minutes, and may therefore prefer to use a visual aid, such as a lighted candle or the yantras (geometric shapes) discussed in the previous chapter. Thus, the whole psychology of the person must first be considered in choosing an appropriate meditation technique and, if necessary, that method should be modified to suit that individual.

Generally speaking, any mental exercise that controls the thought processing system of the brain can be considered a form of meditation, as this often holds the concentration, making one oblivious to all else around.

You can be quite certain that so long as the correct technique of meditation is used the benefits will be experienced at all levels of the practitioner's psychological nature, and may even in the long term effect some profound changes in the individual's situation and circumstances, by encouraging the cultivation of a whole new and more creative approach to life.

The Threefold Meditation Plan is one technique that most people find of great benefit when endeavouring to sharpen the senses. It is a technique that encapsulates the whole person, bringing together the emotional, mental and spiritual aspects of one's nature. It involves three steps: contemplation, concentration and meditation.

As stated above, this technique may not suit everyone, but it can be modified to suit individual meditative requirements, or a more appropriate method can be chosen from the book.

It is always difficult putting something that you are reading actually into practice. Therefore, in order to achieve maximum results from the threefold meditation, you should first of all read through the whole plan a couple of times before actually attempting it. Fix the mental exercises in your mind so that you are completely familiar with the process and do not have to keep referring to the book.

Also, do not be tempted to dismiss the threefold meditation plan because it appears too simple. Actually processing the whole meditation programme is not as easy as it looks. However, once you have mastered the technique you should derive many benefits from it.

THREEFOLD MEDITATION PLAN
Preparation
Begin, as always, with some rhythmic breathing, so as to slow everything down and reduce the level of activity in the mind. Check that your posture is comfortable, ensuring that your back is straight with the shoulders thrown slightly back and your hands are resting lightly on your lap, palms up.

Step One: Contemplation
Focus your thoughts on your reason for meditation, asking yourself what it is that you are seeking to achieve. Try not to make your reason too complicated.

Having decided exactly what it is, establish it fully in your mind, and for five minutes or more contemplate its possibilities. In your contemplative state look at yourself objectively and try to see yourself as others see you. Should the picture you have of yourself reveal someone who is weak and lacking in confidence, change this image into someone who is strong, confident, and even dynamic. Spend some time on this until you have a clear picture of the new you in your mind.

The period of contemplation is used to prepare the mind for the next phase, that of concentration. Concentrating for any length of time can be very tiring, but a few moments spent in contemplation gently brings the meditator into the correct frame of mind, making their ability to concentrate a little sharper.

Step Two: Concentration
Focus the gaze on a point of space in front of you. For a few moments hold it steady, resisting the temptation to blink. When your eyes begin to water, and you can no longer gaze, allow your eyes to close slowly.

At this point you should focus your attention on the top of your head. Allow your attention to penetrate the top of your skull, imagining a small violet, spiralling light, just below the surface of the crown. See it glowing brightly and swirling in a clockwise motion.

Allow your focus to move through the swirling violet light, down to the space just between your brows, and become totally aware of a deep blue pulsating point of light. Allow this to hold your attention for a few moments, and then gradually move your focus inwardly to the throat area. Here you become conscious of a bright blue radiation of light, full of movement and appearing almost luminous. Focus on this for a few moments.

Next, allow your attention to pass inwardly to the region of the heart. Allow yourself to be overwhelmed by a beautiful shade of aquamarine. Feel it quickening your senses. Experience this colour at an emotional level, and then slowly move your focus to the area just below the left side of your ribcage, where you become totally conscious of a sparkling, deep yellow, swirling light. Focus your attention on the yellow light, and be aware of it expanding as it moves in a clockwise motion. Focus on it for a few moments longer, mentally drinking in the vibrant stimulation of the yellow.

Move your attention to the naval area and become aware of a feeling of strength and clarity of thought. Allow your attention to be drawn inside this point and to be overwhelmed by its sheer strength and vitality. Imbibe its power and allow it to circulate around the entire stomach area.

Move slowly to the base of the spine, allowing your attention to be gradually drawn into a fiery glow. Feel the spontaneous energy as your consciousness is drawn deeper into this red, fiery whirlpool, from which you should be conscious of streams of vitality moving up your spine to the crown of your head.

Spend a few moments watching all these beautiful colours individually, before seeing them manifest collectively in a huge pool of colour in front of you. See this swirling pool as though you are standing next to it, watching the sunlight playing across the surface of the water. See the reflection of the sun setting in the centre of the pool. Allow your attention to be drawn down through it, until you feel the colours all around you.

Hold this experience for five or ten minutes before allowing it to dissolve completely from your mind.

Step Three: Meditation
Find yourself sitting at the bottom of a pool, able to breathe and to

see flashes of colour produced by the setting sun above you. Allow your attention to focus on a white lotus flower in front of you, on the bed of the pool. Pick up the flower in cupped hands and see yourself holding it upwards, your arms stretched out towards the cascading light.

Allow yourself mentally to rise to your feet, and see yourself float to the surface of the pond, still holding the beautiful white lotus flower. Allow yourself mentally to emerge into the beautiful light produced by the setting sun and burning like a huge ball of fire on the horizon. Hold the lotus flower up to the fiery sky, which is awash with purple, green, red, yellow and orange flames.

Draw the lotus flower close to your breast, and when you again offer your hands to the sun, see that the lotus flower has been replaced by a white butterfly, which moves off gracefully on the gentle breeze. See its gossamer-like wings, iridescent in the glowing red sunlight, and watch it as it moves away into nothingness.

Sit for a few moments before allowing the meditation to fade gently from your mind, and then relax.

As with all meditations, conclude with some slow, gentle rhythmic breathing. As always, ensure that the inhalations and exhalations are evenly spaced and that you do not make it a labour.

This particular exercise is an experience in colour. As well as having a profound effect on the senses, it helps to clear the auric colours, making them sharper and much more intense.

Through meditation, the mind may exert a greater authority over the aura and the subtle anatomy, and its practice will also encourage the movement of energy through the various channels of vitality.

Activating and releasing the inherent qualities of the individual chakras may be achieved with the use of various mental techniques, such as the yantras and bija-mantras discussed in the last chapter. However, should the use of yantras and bija-mantras not appeal to you in anyway whatsoever, this threefold meditation produces the holistic effect of stabilising the aura and the chakra system.

As with all meditation methods, time should be taken with each part, ensuring that the images created are clearly defined, and that their texture can be felt mentally as well as seen. Allow the images to pass slowly through the mind and make every effort to project your consciousness into the actual situation. Effective meditative techniques take time and practice to achieve but, once you have fully mastered the process, doors to the soul will open and great spiritual heights can then be attained.

CHAPTER TWENTY-TWO
PSYCHIC (PRANIC) HEALING

No book on the aura would be complete without exploring psychic healing, and although many books have been written on this extensive subject, with its many forms and techniques, I would like to explore some of the other methods of healing.

First of all, it is important to point out that the processes of psychic healing and spiritual healing are quite different and should not be confused. Psychic healing is primarily transmitted through the practitioner's aura, and because of this it is essential that the healer's aura is quite healthy and that he or she does not smoke or overindulge in alcohol consumption. A psychic healing practitioner is someone who possesses the ability to draw on large and powerful reservoirs of energy for the purpose of restoring the health and vitality of another person's physical body. Psychic healing is not dependent on faith or religious belief, and the transmutation of incoming energy can also be self-administered. Spiritual healing is a different process entirely and may be administered regardless of the condition of the practitioner's own health, although opinions vary greatly on this matter.

I have already discussed the nature of Prana and explained that it is the subtle agent through which the life of the body is sustained. Therefore, the more Prana that we are able to draw into and store in the body, the higher the quality of our life. A reduction in Prana results in the lowering of our vitality and ultimately a deterioration in the quality of our life. Where there is no Prana there is no life.

Some individuals are able quite naturally to store great amounts of Prana in their bodies, and just being in their presence when we are feeling out of sorts makes us feel much better - uplifted and full of vitality. A person with excellent oratory skills employs great streams of Prana, and is able to draw in and retain these naturally in his or her body. Individuals who have what is called 'charisma' also have streams of Prana pooling their nervous system, and it is this that creates vibrancy in the aura, causing the so-called 'magnetic attraction'. The powers of a successful hypnotherapist only work because he or she has an immense reservoir of Prana and without this the therapy would just not work at all.

The innovator of modern-day hypnotism, Anton Franz Mesmer, observed that whilst he taught all his students the same techniques, phrases and terminology only five out of ten of them proved that they had the ability to promote a hypnotic trance. Mesmer could see that the students who had developed the skill seemed to discharge a radiance, rather like electricity sparking along a bare connection. Mesmer identified this as Prana being discharged from the individual's aura, and he thus concluded that they had Prana stored in great amounts in their bodies.

When a person falls ill, his or her levels of Prana are greatly reduced, but with rest and healthy food the levels of Prana are usually restored, encouraging the health to improve. An individual with psychic healing skills is able to aid a sick person's recovery via a simple process of passing on streams of their own Prana to replenish the invalid's depleted levels. Even in extreme cases of illness, psychic healing can ease pain and alleviate the discomfort experienced.

As I have previously said, Prana is stored in the solar plexus - the so-called 'sun centre', from where it is continually dispensed to the major organs of the physical body. Normally any depletion of Prana in the body is restored through the natural process of atmospheric recharging (breathing), sleep and correct diet, but when the depletion has been long-standing disease becomes apparent. A psychic healer can easily encourage Pranic replenishment with a simple method of rhythmic breathing and transmission of Prana through the fingertips.

PRANIC METHOD ONE
This is a simple experiment to enable you to experience the manifestation of Prana in your hands, so at least then you know exactly what to expect.

* Sit comfortably on a straight-backed chair and place your hands gently on your solar plexus, with your eyes closed.
* Feel the pulse of energy in the abdominal area and allow your hands to remain in this position until you feel the temperature gradually changing.
* If, after five minutes, nothing has happened, shake your hands vigorously for a few minutes, allowing all your fingers to snap together in the process.
* Now place your hands gently on your forehead and feel your fingers tingling with vitality, almost coming alive with energy. As you hold them against your forehead notice how the tingling appears to affect your head, as the fingers discharge streams of Prana into it.
* Once the tingling has ceased, shake your hands vigorously once again for a few moments, and then replace them gently on your solar plexus.
Notice the sensation in your hands. They should feel 'alive' with Prana.

This exercise creates a sudden rush of Prana from the head to the solar plexus. Once you have become accustomed to the feeling of Prana in your hands, you can then more efficiently pass it on to someone else, with the sole intention of making them feel better. Before attempting to pass Prana on to another person, however, it would be a good idea to practise this method of creating Prana a few times until you feel confident that you can do it effectively.

Initially it is advisable to practise the healing process on a friend or family member, so that you don't feel intimidated or pressurised. Working with Prana will also encourage the development of a more confident personality and will help your own health to improve. Creating currents of Prana in your own body gives you more vitality and precipitates a healthier aura. Although most people will not actually 'see' the radiance of your personal bioluminescence, its vibrancy will be felt and will affect all those with whom you come into contact.

Pranic healing is not, generally speaking, a curative method, but it is certainly known to create such movements of energy in the body as to move blockages, thereby encouraging the body's natural self-healing processes. It has quite a powerful effect on pain, and when applied will ease discomfort almost immediately.

PRANIC METHOD TWO

* Seat your patient on a straight-backed chair and stand behind them.
* Close your eyes for a few moments and then place your hands gently on your patient's shoulders, allowing your thoughts to blend completely with theirs.
* Once you have attuned yourself to the patient's body, shake your hands vigorously by your sides for a minute or so, and then point both index fingers towards the floor and imagine streams of energy being drawn up through them.
* With your fingers still extended, slowly raise your hands and place one on either side of the patient's head so that your index fingers are pointing just behind the ears.
* Breathe in slowly and then, as you exhale, mentally discharge the energy from your fingers into the patient's head.
* Repeat this process five or six times, always beginning with the vigorous shaking of your hands, thereby stimulating the flow of Prana.
* Conclude the treatment by positioning your hands to each side of the patient's body and then, without touching them, sweep them up and down the sides from the head down to the hips. Then move to the side of the patient and repeat the sweeping process down their front and back.

If a patient is suffering from some form of infection and has a high temperature, follow the same procedure, but this time visualise the energy that is drawn in through your fingers as being coloured with vibrant blue. When you discharge the energy into the patient's head, again see that it has a powerful blue force as it streams through the fingertips, filling the patient's head completely with the colour of vibrant blue. Should the patient's temperature be low for some reason, use exactly the same method but colour the force red.

The cleansing sweeps of the hands performed at the end of the treatment have a stimulating effect on a person's aura and also encourage the healing force to circulate more efficiently throughout the subtle anatomy. When this treatment is applied on a regular basis, the bioluminescence will improve and achieve a greater clarity.

When a person is recovering from illness and is therefore very low in vitality, the healing processes can be encouraged by the use of a very simple treatment which I call 'auric cleansing'.

This not only has a deep, stimulating effect on the person's energy field, but also helps to encourage movement in the channels that convey energy around the body.

By introducing a little colour into the treatment the person's energy levels are vastly increased, and the whole person (body, mind and spirit) will experience a sudden rush of energy, as though they have been bathed in a powerful beam of cosmic light.

The healer's ability to visualise is extremely beneficial in the transmission of the healing forces and will aid the precipitation of Prana.

PRANIC METHOD THREE
* Ask your patient to lie face down in a horizontal position.
* Place one hand gently on the patient's neck and the other hand at the base of the spine.
* Imagine the spine as a hollow channel, and mentally 'see' each of your hands sparkling with vitality.
* Very slowly move the hand on the neck down the spine, and at the same time move the hand on the base of the spine up towards the head, again mentally 'seeing' both hands sparkling with vitality.
* When both hands meet somewhere in the middle of the patient's back, allow them to remain there alongside each other for a few moments. (Do not allow them to overlap).
* Remove your hands from the patient's back, and with the fingers extended place the right hand over the left one, but not touching each other (as we did in the hand rotating exercise; see page 56).
* Maintaining this position, place the hands over the base of the

spine, approximately an inch away from the body, and begin slowly rotating the left hand in a clockwise motion and the right hand in an anti-clockwise motion.

* Allow the rotating hands to move slowly along the spine, and on reaching the neck follow the same route back towards the base of the spine.

* Repeat this hand rotation process one more time and then, still rotating the hands, move back up the spine until you reach the middle of the back.

* Now part your hands and move one to the base of the spine and the other to the neck, placing them gently in position as at the start of the exercise.

* Keep your hands in their respective positions for a few moments and then remove them. *Look at page 59 for illustration.*

This sort of treatment has a psychological effect on the patient as well as stimulating the entire aura and encouraging the movement of Prana in the chakra system. Although this psychic healing process works primarily at a subtle level, it does produce a beneficial physiological effect when performed regularly.

BREATH, HEAT AND MOVEMENT
Ancient Greek physicians administered healing through the laying on of hands and limb manipulation. Their leading practitioner, Asclepius, carefully breathed on the diseased parts of the body and then applied a gentle rubbing motion with his hands. The ancient Druids also conducted their healing ceremonies in this way, and historical records show that Druid priests were able to cure a wide range of illnesses.

Wise physicians, even among the ancients, have always been aware of how beneficial it is for the blood to make gentle hand movements over the body. This method has been found to be effective with sudden as well as habitual pains and in various forms of debility, being both renovating and strengthening. Today many experienced doctors believe that the heat of the hand is highly beneficial to the sick. Any healing application that brings ease to discomfort of any sort may be regarded as 'psychic'.

CHAPTER TWENTY-THREE
MAGNETIC HEALING
FOR THE AURA

Magnetism is active everywhere, and there is nothing new in it but the name; it is a paradox only to those who ridicule everything, and who attribute to the power of Satan whatever they are unable to explain.

Magnetic healing is another form of Pranic healing and again should not be confused with spiritual healing. This misconception is still harboured today by a lot of people who actually practise magnetic healing in the belief that they are administering spiritual healing.

Magnetic or Pranic healing involves the transmission of a person's own energies, and while there are different theories as to how this process takes place it is an ability we all possess to a greater or lesser degree. Spiritual healing involves a certain degree of attunement with the patient, and also a blending of the healer's mind with a higher power.

In my experience, spiritual healing necessitates some degree of spiritual attainment and discipline but very little technique, while the effectiveness of magnetic or Pranic healing is primarily dependent on ability and technique.

THE BIRTH AND PRINCIPLES OF MAGNETIC HEALING
In the seventeenth century, when the chemist and physician Van Helmont was writing, a Scotsman by the name of Maxwell was practising and teaching the art of magnetic healing. Although this was looked on with some disdain by the Church, Maxwell's belief in a vital spirit that pervaded everything and which could be tapped into to heal the sick caught the imagination of his numerous devotees.

A similar idea surfaced in 1734, when a priest by the name of

Father Hehl propagated the idea of a 'Universal Fluid' that could be used to cure all manner of illnesses. Needless to say, Father Hehl was branded a heretic and driven from the Church.

At the end of the eighteenth century, Friedrich Anton Mesmer, the innovator of mesmerism, the forerunner to hypnotism, taught the radical and unconventional theory of animal magnetism. Initially, he was held in high esteem in Vienna and Paris, and was looked on as a sort of a guru of his day. The Prussian government established a hospital devoted to the application of magnetic healing, and such was the interest in the subject that strict laws were passed by various Continental governments to prevent anyone outside the medical profession from using magnetic treatments. Nonetheless, Mesmer and his ideas fell into disfavour, and some of his followers seized the opportunity to exploit the knowledge they had obtained from him, thus prostituting what they had learned. However, their interpretation of his teachings did give birth to new schools of thought centred around the transference of energy.

HOW MAGNETIC HEALING AFFECTS THE AURA

Although Pranic or magnetic healing is far more effective when administered by a healthy person, someone who is unwell can facilitate the movement of Prana in their own body for the sole purpose of healing themselves. The majority of those studying the subject agree that health problems manifest in the aura some time before they actually become apparent in the physical body. However, to a sceptic this notion will probably seem absurd and regarded as far-fetched and fanciful. Nonetheless, scientific research has proved this to be a fact, and the use of such apparatus as the modern Kirlian camera has now substantiated the claims made by those researching this incredible phenomenon. Experiments with magnetic healing and the aura have proved conclusively that auric fragmentations can be corrected with as few as two treatments. Magnetic passes to the aura appear to polarise it, making it more sharp and vibrant. When the aura is fragmented it can easily be infiltrated by psychic germs, thus lowering its resistance to physical as well as psychological disease. Auric fragmentations often manifest through poor diet, alcohol and nicotine intake as well as wrong thinking. By holistically treating a fragmented aura, leakages may be sealed and the whole person grounded as a result. This process promotes a more balanced individual in body, mind and spirit, thus encouraging a more positive and dynamic attitude to everyday life.

The aura is a sort of a blueprint of the individual it represents, and contains all relevant data about the person's psychological, spiritual and physical make-up. A detailed analysis of the aura will enable you to access an immense store of information and will help you to create a complete psychic profile of the individual. In other words, everything you need to know about a person is contained in his or her personal energy field and may be accessed at any time.

Another effective way of polarising the aura is with the use of metal magnets. Because the aura extends some distance from the body, it is not necessary actually to make physical contact with it, and the next section explains how the magnetic procedure should be implemented.

MAGNETIC HEALING EXERCISE

For the magnetic treatment you will require two metal magnets, large enough to hold comfortably in the hands.

* Take a magnet in each hand, and begin by holding them above the head of your seated patient, about two inches from the head and about three inches from each other.
* Begin the treatment by slowly moving the magnets in opposite directions around the sides of the person's body, working downwards and shaking your hands slightly as they move.
* Take time with the treatment, and when you have reached the hip area follow the same route back up to the top of the head. Repeat this process three times.
* Following the same procedure as before, this time move one magnet down the back of your patient and and one down the front, again taking time with the treatment.

Remember, although you are treating the subtle energies of the aura you are actually using the magnetic properties of two solid objects, therefore no visualisation or mental imagery are necessary for positive results to be achieved.

Once the treatment has been concluded the patient should drink a glass or two of water to hydrate the body. Because the patient's aura has been polarised it is quite normal for them to feel light-headed or even slightly disorientated. However, this should only last until the magnetic polarisation process has taken effect, and everything should be back to normal within five minutes.

It is not necessary to apply this treatment to the entire body, as once the magnetic waves infiltrate the upper part of the aura they are automatically transferred to the other parts of the body.

CHAPTER TWENTY-FOUR
HOW CRYSTALS AFFECT
THE AURA

Although the healing properties of crystals have been extensively covered in the many books on sale today, here I want to make a detailed analysis of what crystals may be used to increase the potential of the aura and how you can best maximise the power of the crystals you use.

The age-old science of crystal power has been found in many cultures throughout the past thousand or so years, but the Ancient Egyptians really believed in crystal magic and frequently took this to the extreme, even orally administering powdered crystals to diseased people. Although this procedure is not recommended, it demonstrates exactly how much these wise Egyptian apothecaries believed in the healing properties of crystals. The potency of each individual crystal produces a specific harmonic effect on the aura, and combinations of crystals, when used in a certain way, will eventually influence the overall tone of the body, thus improving the health.

Today the most popular and probably the most fashionable crystals are amethyst, rose quartz, clear quartz and even lapis lazuli, and these can frequently be seen set in all sorts of items of jewellery. In fact, crystal jewellery pieces are nearly always worn without any knowledge at all of their true healing value and are often just worn as an adornment and fashion accessory. However, whether the wearer is aware of it or not, crystals affect the aura and very often make the wearer feel better - much better. So let's explore the healing powers of crystals and find out what crystals you would derive benefit from.

Firstly we need to consider the chakra system. Do certain crystals affect the individual chakras? Most certainly, and even though traditionally there are crystals that correspond with the seven major chakras, there are others that may be even more beneficial for your chakra system.

The chakras are connected tp the endocrine glands and nerve plexuses through an extensive system of channels called nadis, as already described in Chapter 12. For balance to be maintained in the aura, a consistent flow of energy needs to be encouraged through the chakra system. Although this can be achieved in various ways, crystals directly affect the individual chakras and thus encourage the inherent qualities to be released. Although there are conflicting opinions about which crystals to use on the individual chakras, tabulated below are the seven chakras, the colour traditionally associated with them and crystals that can have a beneficial effect either used individually or in combination:

Chakra	Associated Colour	Connected To	Beneficial Crystal
Muladhara (base)	Red	Physical needs	Bloodstone Haematite Tiger's Eye
Svadhisthana (sacral)	Orange	Emotional security	Carnelian Citrine Golden Topaz
Manipura (solar plexus)	Yellow	Self-control Confidence	Aventurine Quartz Yellow Citrine
Anahata (heart)	Green (Sometimes pale pink)	Love Relationships	Rose Quartz* Tourmaline
Vishudda (throat)	Blue	Auditory faculties	Lapis Lazuli Turquoise

		'Hearing'	Aquamarine
Ajna (brow) (Third Eye)	Indigo	Intuition Perception 'Knowing'	Amethyst** Azurite Fluorite
Sahasrara (crown)***	Violet White (Sometimes gold)	Spirituality Cosmic consciousness	Amethyst Clear Quartz Diamond

* *Rose Quartz works well on its own in providing a powerful infusion of energy*
** *Also known as the spiritual stone*
*** *Due to the position of this chakra, the crystal(s) should be placed on the floor as close to the crown of the head as possible*

CRYSTAL HEALING TREATMENT

Simply lie in a comfortable horizontal position and position the appropriate crystals carefully on the corresponding chakras. The process is very often enhanced by playing some soft, relaxing music and also by burning pleasant oils or incense. This encourages the psychological aspects and helps to promote calmness, a prerequisite for the whole treatment.

Whilst this holistic treatment requires nothing other than for you to relax, a little visualisation will encourage the process and facilitate the precipitation of energies.

Visualisation

Simply focus your attention on the individual chakras in turn, beginning with the area on the crown of the head. See an intense point of white light directly on the crystal, and then mentally move the light down from the crown to the area between your brows. Stop for a few moments at each crystal, and imagine the light spiralling around in a clockwise motion at each point. Follow the route of the crystals down to the base of the spine, pause for a moment, and then mentally move the intense white light along the same route back towards the crown of the head.

Conclude the exercise by sitting quietly with your eyes closed, holding a piece of amethyst in your upheld, cupped hands. Feel the pulse of the crystal, and then mentally see the amethyst's violet light slowly moving around your whole body. Visualise the violet energy enveloping your body completely, energising and revitalising your body, mind and spirit. Finally, hold the amethyst gently to your forehead and feel its power inside your head. Hold it in that position for a few moments and then relax with it on your lap.

Many people would disregard the concept of crystal healing as being far-fetched and fanciful, but it would be quite foolish to dismiss it until you have tried it for yourself. Having used crystals a lot over the years, I have found that some work for me and others do not. I do know there is a great deal of nonsense written about crystals and the way in which they should be used. I have found that certain stones do have a very strong resonance with some people, whilst other people are completely unaffected by them. Let's take amethyst as an example: the majority of those being treated with crystals find the very beautiful deep shade of the amethyst therapeutic in itself. Even the visually handicapped person responds well to treatment with amethyst, so I know it is not just the psychological influence of the colour of the stone itself. As I have previously said, amethyst is regarded as the 'spiritual stone', and does have quite a powerful effect on the aura. In fact, the overall appearance of the aura improves greatly after treatment with amethyst, and even its bioluminescence appears much more radiant too. This suggests that amethyst most certainly affects the electromagnetic radiance of the body by introducing into it some of its own powerful qualities. Just to sit quietly with a nice piece of amethyst for ten minutes or so encourages the mind to be quiet and produces an overall feeling of serenity and calm. By introducing some visualisation into the process, a greater release of the amethyst's qualities is encouraged.

AMETHYST VISUALISATION EXERCISE

This exercise affects the chakras as well as the aura, and also helps to encourage a more positive and relaxed attitude towards life generally. It is important not to allow your mind to drift from the visualisation even for a moment, and that the imagery is consistently maintained for the whole of the meditation.

Sit in a comfortable position with a piece of amethyst resting in the palms of your upturned hands, close your eyes and imagine you have a lotus of a thousand petals resting gently on the top of your head. See yourself in a beautiful meadow of lush green grass, with a blue, cloudless sky surrounding the sun, which is very bright and clear in your mind. As you see the sun burning brightly in the clear blue sky, imagine the sunlight is suddenly transformed into a beam of intense white light that streams down through the centre of the lotus flower on the top of your head. Feel the stream of intense white light piercing the lotus, filling your head completely with energy and light. Watch the white light moving slowly from your head down to your shoulders and then following a straight route on its descent to the lowest part of your spine. Spend a few minutes watching the white light streaming from your head and down your spine, from where it moves down each of your legs. Not only see the intense white light, but try to feel it too.

Maintain the imagery for at least ten minutes, and then see the intense white light gradually fade until it disappears completely. Once again, be aware of the green lush grass all around you. See the bright sun in a clear, cloudless blue sky, and feel its warm rays on your face. This time imagine the sun's golden rays cascading down through the centre of the lotus resting on the top of your head. See the powerful golden light filling your head completely, and then watch it gradually moving from your head to your shoulders. See the golden light moving slowly down your spine, and then down each of your legs to your feet. Once again, spend a few minutes watching and feeling the golden light circulating around your head, spine and legs.

Conclude the visualisation process by seeing the golden light rushing upwards from your feet, up your legs and spine, and finally moving out through the centre of the lotus up towards the sun. Relax for a few moments, and be aware of the green grass all around you and the bright sun in a cloudless blue sky. Allow the green of the grass to envelop you. See yourself completely surrounded by bright green light. Feel it against your skin, energising your body and your mind. Then allow the green light to dissolve.

Next be aware of the blue sky. Allow the blue of the sky to be drawn down like a huge blanket of blue light. See yourself surrounded completely by blue light and feel it against your body. Slowly draw the blue vibrant energy through the centre of the lotus on top of your head. Allow the blue energy to circulate your body for a few seconds. Feel it stimulating every cell in your body and soothing away all the tension from your body and from your mind. Now see the powerful blue light streaming up your legs and spine, and then moving quickly through the centre of the lotus on the top of your head.

Finally, still relaxed, focus all your attention on the amethyst in your hands and feel its energy moving slowly up your arms to your shoulders. Now see the amethyst's deep, resonating energy filling your head completely. Hold it there for as long as possible, and then watch the amethyst's deep purple energy as it streams out through the centre of the lotus on the top of your head and returns to the amethyst held gently in your lap. Feel the amethyst vibrating in your hands. Hold it for a few moments and then breathe in slowly and deeply, and as you breathe out slowly dissolve the exercise from your mind. When you are ready open your eyes.

Regardless of how simple you think the visualisation exercise is, it should still be taken seriously as a psychological process of cleansing the aura. In fact, the energies of the aura respond extremely well to mental stimuli, and the aura as a whole is a complete database containing every detail about the individual to whom it belongs. The way we think is registered in its own aspect of the aura, as are the ways we eat and feel. As I have previously said, the aura is a blueprint of everything you are, everything you have done, and everything you are likely to do in the future. Not only do you carry your personal space around with you everywhere, but you also leave traces of it everywhere you have been. It is this phenomenon that allows others to obtain information about you in your absence. Although individually we are continually creating our own personal space, collectively we are creating the aura of the world - the environment of our future planet.

CHAPTER TWENTY-FIVE
THE SCIENCE OF THE
OUT-OF-BODY EXPERIENCE

We hear a great deal these days about out-of-body experiences (OBEs). Claims are made by some that they have found themselves floating outside their physical body, which they could see below them, either fast asleep in bed, or even lying on an operating table surrounded by a medical team, undergoing surgery.

Many such experiences have been documented over the last 20 years or so, involving people from many different walks of life, many cultures, and with diverse religious beliefs, from the elderly right down to very young children. Some of the accounts recorded have been given by people who allegedly have had no prior knowledge of such a phenomenon.

Even though much of the information contained within the accounts of out-of-body experiences differs in various ways, all the accounts have a common thread running through them which binds them together in some way, thereby adding credence to the claims made.

Although most of the experiences have occurred mainly when the body is anaesthetised, there have been accounts of this unusual phenomenon taking place quite spontaneously while the person was fully awake. When an individual experiences the phenomenon in such a spontaneous way, he or she can be left in very little doubt that it has occurred while they were fully awake. However, overactivity of the imagination can only be eliminated when the out-of-body experience has been put to the test, and it must be said that six out of ten cases fail this test miserably, even though it is quite straightforward. The person is simply asked to relate what they observed during the out-of-body experience that they otherwise would not have seen had their consciousness remained in the physical body. Furthermore, the person experiencing such a phenomenon also demonstrates a heightened state of awareness of everything around them, so their consciousness is somehow able to transcend the limitations of the physical body to perceive a fuller geographical landscape, for example allowing them to experience things taking place in an adjacent road or room or, in some rarer cases of the phenomenon, even in a different part of the world. One other commonality is that they find the experience extremely pleasant and something that they would very much like to replicate.

Before we explore certain techniques that allow this phenomenon to be produced, we must first of all look at the reasons why it happens at all, and also make a detailed analysis of the whole concept of the out-of-body phenomenon and its possibilities.

Even though the out-of-body experience may be considered a very natural phenomenon, it cannot in any way be thought of as 'normal', and it is certainly not the sort of event one experiences every day of the week. Although it is a phenomenon that can be indicative of certain psychological and emotional illnesses, it is not, strictly speaking, symptomatic of anything in particular. It is certainly a phenomenon that is being widely studied today, and one over which modern psychologists seem to be more or less split in their opinions, although nearly all are in agreement that such a phenomenon does indeed take place. One notable neurologist has devoted four years of his life to researching the whole concept of the out-of-body experience, and he has now concluded that the evidence is far too extensive to ignore. He also believes that the thousands of cases he has looked at during his research suggest the possibility of some form of life beyond death.

Before we explore the out-of-body experience, we must firstly work on the premise that man not only possesses some form of astral body in the first place but also that he himself is an extremely complex being, possessing other more subtle bodies through which his consciousness can also move and have an experience. In theory, man at any time can experience awareness of any of these bodies, and sometimes does, without actually realising it. For example, consider a soldier in the grip of attack behind enemy lines. His consciousness is completely focused on the approaching enemy and the battle at hand, and he does not notice that he has been wounded. Once the battle is over and the enemy has withdrawn, his consciousness once again moves to his physical body and, realising that he has been injured, he falls into unconsciousness. During the time the soldier's consciousness was preoccupied, he experienced awareness in one of his astral counterparts, thus making the physical body completely anaesthetised to all sensation and oblivious to anything but the approaching danger. Although an extremely simple analogy, it is, I feel, one that illustrates the concept of shifting consciousness perfectly well.

Another example relates to what is experienced in deep sleep when one is dreaming. Here again the sleeper is completely oblivious to both his body and his surroundings, and experiences awareness in a state of consciousness over which he appears to have little or no control. If the sleeper were able to control his consciousness during the time he were asleep, there would be limitless possibilities and greater freedom of awareness available to him. By developing control of the consciousness, particularly during sleep, man would be able to access states of awareness in which time and space as we conceive them would simply not exist. I am, of course, speaking of the 'subjective' levels of the astral world, in which the geography is peculiar to that part of the astral universe alone and in no way bears any relation to the geography of the physical world. In sleep we lose all spatial limitations, and the consciousness is able to transcend the bounds of time as well as space. It is a fact that most of our psychic experiences occur either during the hypnogogic state (in between being awake and falling asleep) or the hypnopompic state (in between being asleep and waking up). These altered states of consciousness happen quite naturally when we are tired and getting ready to sleep. However, when we have been anaesthetised (as in the case of surgery), the altered states of consciousness are artificially induced, and so the astral body is forced to move through different states of consciousness, which is quite often why out-of-body experiences are actually remembered as much as they are.

Because of the very nature of the astral world, until one develops the ability of the consciousness to function with more controlled freedom, one's sensory awareness of the astral world can only be described as nebulous. However, once such development takes place, it is as though a grey veil rises to reveal before the consciousness a new and vibrant landscape of colour, form and sound.

Various techniques can be employed in order to project the astral body, but before any of these are explored it is important to learn to focus the consciousness on the self and this can be achieved with the following simple meditative exercise.

FOCUSING THE CONSCIOUSNESS EXERCISE
Step One
Sit comfortably, preferably on a straight-backed chair, with your back straight and hands resting lightly on your lap. Breathe slowly and deeply, making quite sure that the inhalations and exhalations are evenly spaced. Quieten the mind as much as possible and relax your body. Remain in this position for a few minutes until you feel quite serene and totally relaxed. When you feel ready, physically rise from your chair and walk into an adjacent room.

Make a mental note of everything you can see there, creating a clear picture in your mind so that you know where everything is and can recall the details in your imagination later. Now return to your chair in your quiet room and relax once again with your eyes closed. Begin to breathe slowly and deeply, summoning all the power you can into your solar plexus. Discharge this power on the exhalations, whilst creating in your mind a clear image of yourself standing in front of you and facing away, so that you have a clear view of your own back.

Try to see yourself clearly, dressed in the same clothes that you are wearing now, and watch yourself walking away towards the door. When you can see yourself reaching the door, freeze the image of yourself, breathe in deeply, and on the exhalation allow the image of yourself to fade.

Step Two

Rise from your chair and wander once again into the adjacent room. Repeat the motions of looking round and checking the position of everything in the room. Use all your senses to record the full picture accurately. Familiarise yourself with any fragrance, pay attention to colours, and make a special note of the exact position of items of furniture. In other words, refresh your mental picture of exactly how everything looks. Return to your chair in your quiet room and relax again, with your eyes closed.

Breathe slowly and deeply once more, paying attention to the streams of vitality flowing in through your nostrils and down into your solar plexus. Try to become accustomed to breathing in this way, summoning all the power you can into your solar plexus. Remember, as you breathe in let your stomach rise and when you breathe out let it fall. Each time you exhale, discharge the power, and simultaneously recreate the image of yourself standing in the doorway ready to leave. See yourself passing through the door and out of sight.

Still totally relaxed, imagine yourself now as the image you have created of yourself. Allow yourself mentally to move into the adjacent room. Once there, stand for a few moments and look around. Feel as though you are actually there: smell the fragrances, see the colours of everything around you, and note the position of the furniture. Move about in the room, allowing your eyes to scan your surroundings, before slowly moving back towards the door. Stand in the doorway for a few moments and take a last look around before leaving the room and returning to your chair.

Before opening your eyes, sit quietly for a few moments, breathing gently and rhythmically. When you feel ready to conclude the exercise, breathe in deeply one last time and with the exhalation discharge the whole picture from your mind. Then open your eyes.

Once you have finished this exercise, it is vitally important not to go over it in your mind. Instead, direct your mind completely away from it and make yourself a warm drink.

Even if your powers of imagination are extremely good, little will be accomplished from one or even two sittings. To achieve full astral projection the experiment must be conducted over and over until very little concentration is needed on your part, and the imagery pulls you along automatically, of its own accord, and not the other way around. When this happens you will know it. The imagery you create in your mind will suddenly become intensified and you will experience a pleasant feeling of floating. This is the all -important point at which the astral body seeks separation. When this sensation is experienced many people become excited, which has the effect of inhibiting the process so that it simply does not progress any further. Therefore, once you experience this sensation of buoyancy, try to remain completely calm and relaxed. Should this prove difficult - the excitement and anticipation are often extremely difficult to contain - it is quite acceptable to suspend the exercise until later, when you have had some time to reflect objectively on what has happened.

Remember, full projection does take time and a lot of practice. However, once it has been confidently achieved, the boundaries can be extended. Arrangements can be made to travel astrally to the home of a friend with whom you feel comfortable and who you can trust, someone who lives only a short distance away. Remember, the experiment must still be carried out in the same way, and the exact same procedure must be followed.

Apart from the obvious projection of the astral body, these visualisation methods exercise the image-making faculty of the brain, encouraging a more intensified aura. Learning to control the mind with the use of these techniques also precipitates the consciousness and cultivates a more heightened state of sensory perception.

Step Three
Take a casual stroll to your friend's house, making a mental note of everything you can see on your journey: the other houses and the way in which they are painted, the gardens, the traffic, children playing in the street and even people passing by. In other words, mentally record everything so that you can recall it clearly in your imagination later on. Make the journey several times if

necessary before beginning the exercise.

Once you have arranged everything with your friend, return to your home and sit quietly, relaxing as completely as you possibly can. When you feel ready and the exercise has been established fully in your mind, follow it in your imagination in exactly the same way as you did with the previous experiment, going slowly through it stage by stage, until you feel confident that the imagery you have made of yourself is now strong enough to commence the journey to your friend's home.

Should your attention wander at some point whilst visualising yourself making the short journey to your friend's house, imagine yourself walking back to your own home, passing through your front door and returning to your chair, and suspend the exercise until later.

You may initially like to consider not completing the exercise in one sitting. It is quite acceptable to go through it in stages, possibly splitting the journey: (1) seeing yourself moving to your front door; (2) going as far as the garden gate; (3) walking a few yards from your house; (4) walking halfway down the street; (5) reaching your friend's front door; and (6) entering your friend's home and walking into the room where he or she is sitting.

It may all sound fairly straightforward and simple, but believe me it is not. This technique calls for a great deal of practice, patience and total dedication. It may, of course, take you a comparatively short time to achieve full astral projection. It all depends on your ability to project your imagination and on the latent potential that you already possess. You may even experience projection spontaneously, without going through the whole procedure of visualisation. On the other hand, it may well take you a long time to achieve. Whichever category you fall into, try not to lose interest, and make sure you practise as often as possible, as this is the only way in which results can be positively and successfully achieved.

Once you have successfully projected your imagination to your friend's house, you must mentally make a note of everything you can see. Mentally scan your surroundings, observe what your friend is doing, and register everything that is going on in the

143

room where he or she is sitting. When the exercise has been concluded, you must compare notes with your friend, so that everything you report can be confirmed.

This sort of exercise is also extremely beneficial for anyone suffering from agoraphobia - the fear of open spaces. It is an extremely effective tool for cultivation of the imagination and expansion of the aura. The more your powers of visualisation are used, the stronger and more defined your aura will become.

CHAPTER TWENTY-SIX
COLOUR HEALING
AND THE AURA

The concept of colour healing has been around for thousands of years, and even as far back as when the pyramids were being erected in Ancient Egypt, colour was being used to heal maladies of both the body and the mind. The Ancient Egyptian colour therapists used muslin-like cloth in different colours, which they used to filter the sun's rays. The patient would be seated beneath alternating coloured filters, and would remain there for long periods whilst being bathed in the various powerful coloured rays.

Although now a lot more advanced, colour healing is today still considered an extremely effective way of restoring the health and maintaining balance in the body. Colour healing holistically infiltrates the aura and encourages a more even distribution of colour, thus sharpening the overall bioluminescence of the aura. Even though the method is different, the theory behind it is still very much the same as it was all those thousands of years ago.

The cause of feeling continually under the weather may be something as simple as the colour arrangement in the home, and a colour makeover may not only encourage health improvements but also may even brighten the way you think about everything. Living in a dismally decorated home is not only extremely depressing but also in the long term will have a profound effect on one's overall health. Even constantly wearing our favourite colours can have an effect on psychological as well as physical well-being. Although done completely unconsciously, most people tend to like wearing colours that are usually present in their aura in great amounts. The vibratory resonance of the colours we wear produces an extremely powerful effect on our aura, and can either uplift us or make us feel completely out of sorts.

The age-old saying, 'Feeling in the pink', means far more than you might imagine. When pink is seen in a person's aura it not only shows that they are quite emotional and feeling, but also when seen in flashes through the entire aura it shows that the individual is feeling happy and 'on top of the world'. In fact, experiments conducted in a secure psychiatric unit in California some years ago were fairly conclusive about the effects of colour on some patients. A severely ill man who could just about function when highly medicated had all his medication withdrawn for the purpose of the experiment. He very quickly showed all the symptoms of someone with his acute mental illness, and became incoherent, confused and very agitated. He was then placed in a completely pink room, with pink lights constantly burning, and within half an hour the young man became quite calm and coherent and showed significant signs of recovery. Of course, the mental equilibrium achieved was not permanent, and when he was removed from the pink therapy room his medication had to be reintroduced.

Similar experiments were conducted involving visually handicapped patients. Although they were not able actually to 'see' the colours with which they were being treated, they were able to say whether the colours made them feel warm or cold, relaxed or full of energy. This experiment enabled the researchers to understand the vibrational value of colour more fully, and led them to conclude that colour affected the body as well as the mind.

Although we have explored the various auric colours and their meanings, the concept of colour healing is completely different. We all know how we feel after taking a leisurely walk in the countryside on a warm summer's afternoon, or how we feel after spending some time at the seaside. As well as the fresh, invigorating air, the natural colours of nature also saturate our minds with vitality and infuse our auras with energy. Green is the colour of balance and is an extremely vibratory energy for the heart. The vibrations of green are also effective in healing the emotions or the stressed mind.

The clear blue of the sky is a powerful healing colour that encourages the body's natural healing processes, and is a calming vibration for the nervous system. Blue is also an ideal colour for soothing inflammation or painful diseases. In fact, the psychological effect of colour encourages the self-healing processes of the mind. We all know only too well how we physically feel when we are ecstatically happy and in a state of euphoria. It causes the body to be anaesthetised to feeling and any previously felt pain magically disappears. Happiness and joy encourage a release of endorphins, the brain's natural painkillers, which attaches to the same cell receptors as morphine, allowing the body to deal with pain. Some colours have a powerful effect on the brain, encouraging its resistance against disease and inflammation.

Although wearing certain colours is quite beneficial to the body and to the mind, the healing process is not quite the same as surrounding yourself with vibrant colours, as in the decor of your home. An even more effective method is to bathe yourself in a powerful coloured light for a short period of time. In fact, it is possible to obtain a special light box in which a coloured crystal or slide can be placed. I personally found the light intensity of these ineffective and so I adapted an old slide projector. In some cases I used various pieces of coloured acetate in the projector, and when more power was required I used slides to which I stuck minute grains of coloured crystal. Apart from everything else, the psychological effects of this coloured light treatment are quite powerful and it also produces remarkable curative effects on the physical body. Although you can purchase a special chromatherapy lamp for the colour transmission, ordinary electric lamps with 200 watt bulbs will sometimes suffice. Likewise, if it is not possible to use infrared and ultraviolet lamps, simultaneous use of red and blue bulbs is nearly always just as effective. As with all complementary treatments, however, no guarantees can or should be given, and the results are solely dependent on the severity of the condition as well as the co-operation of the patient.

When treating someone with colour therapy it is always a good idea to be guided intuitively when trying to decide which colours to use. If you are used to working with people, you should be able to 'feel' what colours are lacking. Sometimes all that is required when treating the aura with colour therapy is a sort of general tonic with a small assortment of colours, rather like taking a multivitamin. This has a 'washing down' effect on the aura and makes the person feel as though they have had a powerful tonic.

Colour healing can also be mentally transmitted to a patient, and with this method of treatment no physical contact is required.

To give you a much clearer understanding of what colours to use, you may like to study the list below. The more you learn about the colours and how they affect the body and mind, the more you may want to improvise and even create combinations of colours to produce the maximum effect.

Colour	Conditions Affected/Purpose
Red	Any condition related to the blood; an energiser
Blue	Migraine and other headaches, fevers, cancer, burns, rheumatism
Blue and purple	High blood pressure
Purple	Low blood pressure
Indigo	Blood impurities, muscle weakness, poor body tone, boils, acne
Violet	Bone growth, lung congestion, stress, anxiety
Violet and indigo	Heart problems, cancer, some stomach problems
Green	Head colds, hay fever, lung problems such as congestion and pneumonia, psychic problems, poor eyesight, liver disorders, obesity, malaria, typhoid
Green and red	Sluggish nervous system, lethargy, liver disorders
Yellow	Tuberculosis and other lung problems
Yellow and green	Nervous disorders, some psychological problems
Orange	Lung problems, lack of confidence
Orange and bright red	Exhaustion; a general tonic for the whole person
Yellow and blue	Mental disorders
Violet, lavender and	

deep orange	Anxiety, stress, hyperactivity of the mind
Blue and violet	Psychological and psychic problems; holistic
Green and blue	Sciatica, inflammatory diseases
Yellow and orange	Kidney and liver problems; stimulates whole body
Blue, green and orange	Imbalances in the body and chakra system
Violet and red	Infuses the chakra system with vitality and produces a 'sweeping' effect across the aura
Yellow and blue	Insanity, depression; helps to stimulate underactive chakras
Red, yellow and blue	Encourages an even flow of Prana through the subtle anatomy, and precipitates an even distribution of Prana in the aura

The above gives just a small number of colours and combinations to give you some idea how they can be used when treating a person's aura, although it must be pointed out that they may simply have no effect on some people. Experimentation is the best way to reach your own conclusions about what colours to use and how long to use them for. As I have already said, you must allow your intuition to guide you when making your choice of colours, and it is also important to keep a record of how the person you are treating responds to each colour you use. In order to achieve maximum results from the colour treatment, suggestions may also need to be made regarding colour changes to a person's home decor or clothes. For instance, although it can be quite fashionable to wear black or other dark colours, the vibratory rate of black encourages negative emotions and can draw negative forces from other individuals towards the wearer. Conversely, white or other light colours reflect heat and will also reflect negative emotions away from the wearer.

We are greatly affected by our surroundings and the colours we live with, and the psychological effects of dark and dismal colours can be quite powerful and even influence you to behave completely out of character. So, if in doubt, choose white. All colours evolve from white, and white is the highest colour, the colour of spiritual power.

CHAPTER TWENTY-SEVEN
THE AURA OF
ENVIRONMENT

Although we touch thousands of objects during the course of the day, we only have a superficial encounter with the things with which we make contact. Nonetheless, we do impregnate every object we encounter with our own personal energies, and those energies remain 'locked' in the overall structure of everything we have touched. Even the environment in which we live represents us in our absence and replicates our emotional and psychological natures combined. We psychically contribute to the subtle materials from which our environment is created, just as much as we are responsible for the overall subtle feelings emanating from the bricks and mortar of the house in which we live. A person who is kind and well meaning will not remain for very long in the company of a wicked and totally unpleasant individual, any more than you would continue to live out your life in a house with a cold and evil feeling. Depending on whether there is sympathetic resonance, a person's aura either attracts or repels other people, in the same way that an unpleasant district instinctively forewarns you not to go there.

I have previously described the aura as a vaporous mass of electromagnetic particles, surrounding both animate and inanimate matter, and explained that the cells that comprise your body create the chemical phenomenon we know as bioluminescence, the radiant glow of the aura that surrounds you. Your aura 'feels' another person long before you actually physically make contact with them and, as well as being a blueprint of your life on all levels, your aura also functions as a sort of a radar screen, constantly scanning your environment in search of danger.

The mind is an extremely complex mechanism and functions in close proximity to the aura, a powerful combination capable of accessing incredible subtle dimensions of energy. The innumerable waves of thought we create during our lifetime attract and are attracted by thoughts of a sympathetic nature. They form thought strata in the psychic environment, in very much the same way that clouds fall into groups in the atmosphere. However, this does not mean that each stratum of thought occupies a portion of space to the exclusion of all other thought clouds. On the contrary, each particle of thought matter is made up of different degrees of vibration, and so the same space may be filled with thought matter of many different kinds, passing freely and interpenetrating each other without interference. Thus, the subtle environment in which you live has been created by all those who live or have lived there throughout the years, and this either attracts or repels those who attempt to live within its confines.

A sensitive would quite naturally 'feel' the atmosphere, either finding it welcoming or being instinctively repelled by it. Cities, countries and even nations are permeated by the thought environment that has been created by all those who live and have lived there over the past hundreds and even thousands of years. Famine, war and hostile emotions are perpetuated by the anguish and terror created by all those who dwell within the confines of the environment, and these become stronger and more vibrant as they are infused with even more corresponding thoughts, similar to those from which it was created in the first place.

In the same way that we can mentally 'home-in' to psychically assess an environment, we can also mentally access information contained in an artefact that once belonged to someone else. Psychometry is a method of psychically monitoring the historical information of an article, such as a item of jewellery, by simply holding it gently between the fingers. Although psychometry does not work immediately for everyone, with patience and a lot of practice results will be achieved.

PSYCHOMETRY EXPERIMENT

For this exercise you will require an item of jewellery belonging to a member of your friend's family (so that he or she can confirm the information you give). Your friend should also have a notepad and pen to jot down the information you glean from the artefact.

* Hold the article gently between your fingers and sit quietly with your eyes closed.
* Using both hands and as many fingers as possible, take plenty of time to assess each of the item's qualities, such as weight, shape, texture and even temperature.
* Mentally, carefully monitor all the feelings and impressions you receive from the item of jewellery, allowing them to be processed through the mental screen of your mind. Do not dwell on any of the impressions, but for the time being simply make a mental note of all the things you feel.
* When one particular impression seems to stand out, regardless of what it is, tell your friend. Initially you may only receive simple impressions, such as numbers, faces or fragrances, but no matter what you see or feel you must share it with your friend.
* During this process, neither you nor your friend should analyse any of the information gleaned from the item of jewellery.
* Spend no longer than fifteen minutes on the exercise, and when you have finished your assessment put the article down.
* If you have been fairly successful, your friend should notice some sort of connection between all the things you have gleaned. Some of the information may not be connected to the item of jewellery at all, but may be associated with someone else in your friend's family.

The process of psychometry is an ideal tool for sharpening the faculty responsible for clairvoyance, and the more it is used the stronger it will become.

Psychometry is a method of divination used by many clairvoyants to glean information about someone either living or dead. Once you have successfully developed the skill of gleaning information from a small artefact, the ability may also be used to process information from something much larger. In fact, some psychometrists simply use their minds to process information, and just looking at something is all they need to do in order to obtain the psychic data.

Psychometry is an extremely efficient method for obtaining information, and once the skill has been fully developed anything whatsoever may be used as a psychometric focal point.

CHAPTER TWENTY-EIGHT
ASTROLOGICAL INFLUENCES
ON THE AURA

Most people are curious to know what their future holds, and will even check their horoscope in the daily newspaper or a magazine to see how their week is going to go. Some people carry this curiosity to the extreme by consulting an astrologer to have their personal chart drawn up, and will not make a business decision unless the chart says it is all right to do so. Even a sceptic will have some fascination with the unknown, and there is nothing more unknown than our own futures. However, apart from the popular divinatory aspects of astrology, the movement of the planets in the heavens can produce a more significant effect on our lives by encouraging changes in the polarity of our aura.

Although a pseudoscience, the study of the position and movement of the sun, moon, stars and planets may also enable us to calculate our individual energy levels and to understand more fully why on some days we function more efficiently than on others.

Modern-day devotees of astrology make every effort to integrate ancient conjectures into the more scientific concepts and believe that the ever-changing patterns of the planets in the heavens are the primary cause of the variations in the Earth's magnetic field. This magnetic phenomenon influences the neural circuits of our brains, and as a consequence causes significant changes in the polarity of our aura. Although this is not a traditionally accepted concept, extraterrestrial events do affect the human psyche and thus exert a much more powerful influence on our lives than is generally accepted by science.

It would seem that some astrological signs are affected far more than others, and that these signs even experience periods of deep depression as a consequence of the magnetic influence of the moon and other planets. The three water signs - Cancer, Pisces and Scorpio - seem to be affected by these planetary positions far more than other astrological signs. These three water signs are regarded as the most sensitive and emotional of all the astrological signs and are therefore the most receptive. It would also seem that the negative effects of this magnetic planetary phenomenon are neutralised when those born under these signs live close to water. The air signs - Libra, Aquarius and Gemini - are next to be affected and, although the effects on these signs appear not to be quite as severe, the head is still greatly affected, and women more than men very often suffer with headaches as a consequence. The planetary effects are neutralised when these signs live in the countryside.

The earth signs - Virgo, Taurus and Capricorn - tend to be more grounded and earthy and, although generally speaking those born under these signs are stronger and more resilient, the magnetic pull of the planets may cause disorientation and lack of motivation. Living close to woodland or by lots of trees will greatly ease the problem. The fire signs - Aries, Leo and Sagittarius - tend to become irrational, impulsive and behave completely out of character when influenced by the magnetic waves of the planets. These signs also find great relief either in open spaces or in hilly terrain.

PROTECTING THE AURA FROM MAGNETIC INFLUENCE
There are two very different ways of normalising the aura when it has been affected by the magnetic pull of the planets. Either method can be used at any time as a 'pick-me-up' when you are feeling sluggish or just out of sorts.

Polarising the Aura - Method One
For this exercise you will need several small magnets.

* Attach four magnets in some way to your belt - two at the front and two at the back. Then place one magnet in your shirt pocket, and attach one to each ankle. This may sound a bit bizarre, but it is a powerful method that polarises the aura fairly quickly.

* Lie in a relaxed position, ensuring that your hands are resting lightly on your tummy.
* Close your eyes and breathe rhythmically until the rhythm is fully established.
* Remain in this horizontal position for at least twenty minutes.
* To conclude the exercise, sit on your heels with your legs bent at the knees and your hands clasped in front of you.
* Remain in this position, breathing slowly and deeply and with your eyes closed, for a further ten minutes.
* Remove the magnets from your body and have a cool glass of water.

It is a good idea to repeat this exercise twice a day, once in the morning and once late afternoon, if this is possible, for a period of three consecutive days.

Usually positive results are experienced after the first session. You may experience a feeling of slight disorientation, but this should only last a very short time. You may also experience a feeling of exhilaration, almost as though you had taken a brisk walk in the countryside.

The magnets encourage a more stabilised aura and help to improve the general circulation of vitality. Although extremely therapeutic, treatment with the magnets should only be administered for a short period, and most certainly should not be performed for any longer than suggested above.

Polarising the Aura - Method Two
Should you prefer a less radical method, this simple visualisation technique will most probably suit you better.

Sit in a comfortable chair or, if you prefer, lie in a horizontal position with your head resting gently on a cushion or pillow and then, with your eyes closed, start to breathe rhythmically, ensuring that the inhalations and exhalations are evenly spaced and that you do not make the process of breathing a labour. Once you are fully relaxed, you can commence the following visualisation:

See yourself floating in a gradually ascending way towards the deep blue of space. Allow your ascent to be very slow and gradual, and the higher you ascend the more blue you can see surrounding you.

When you feel as though you have ascended high enough into the blue of space, imagine you can see yourself surrounded by distant planets. See them turning about you in space, and notice that each planet is radiating a thin beam of intense white light, that streams towards you. Feel the intense white light gently caressing your skin, and as it does your whole body tingles as though touched by electrical currents. Maintain the imagery, as though you are watching it all on a screen in front of you. Continue to see the planets clearly rotating slowly about you, each one silhouetted by the deep blue of space. Maintain this picture in your mind, moving your consciousness from one planet to another, and then from all the planets to the blue of space.

As soon as you feel that you have had enough, allow yourself to descend through the blue of the space surrounding you. See the planets receding into the distance as you descend even further. Allow all the imagery to fade slowly from your mind, and then feel yourself lying there, very relaxed and calm.

Conclude the exercise with some slow rhythmic breathing. Then finally, as you breathe out, dissolve the entire exercise completely from your mind. Remain in the horizontal position with your eyes closed for a few moments longer and then open your eyes and have a nice cold drink of water.

This visualisation method revitalises the aura and encourages it to be realigned. In fact, unlike the previous exercise with the magnets, this method can be used as often as you like without any adverse effects.

CONCLUDING COMMENTS

Learning to understand and work with the aura may take some time and a lot of practice. This depends solely on the inherent awareness you already have within you. You may well find that you have an aptitude for seeing and working with the aura, and therefore require very little training. Should this be the case then you will know almost immediately. As I have said in the earlier part of this book, the aura is far more than a descriptive term. It is a scientific fact - a metaphysical phenomenon. Cultivating a stronger and more refined aura will enable you to gain greater control of your life. It will give you more insight into your own nature and enable you to better understand the world around you. Working with your aura will help you to eliminate negative patterns of thinking and to adopt a more positive approach to any difficulties you encounter. The more aware you become of the aura, the more sensitive you will become to the environment around you. As a direct consequence of your knowledge of the aura, you will be more able to sense and see the intricate and wonderful patterns through every aspect of life.

I frequently sit at my bedroom window and watch the sun setting on the Dee Estuary not very far my home. This breathtaking view is like gazing through a portal to another world. In reality, though, it is really just the way my consciousness translates the images that my eyes have taken in, things the majority of people most probably take for granted. Having been psychic since I was a child, I grew up being able to see, with great ease, the swirling multicoloured mist around things and people. Trees particularly hold the greatest fascination for me, as they seem to emanate the most interesting energies. In fact, trees are extremely easy to work with, particularly in the early stages of the development of auric visions. Just relax your eyes and focus your stare gently on a tree with its silhouette against the sky. You will see with great ease, the very pale blue energy completely surrounding the tree's foliage. The more you gaze at it the more extensive the energy will become. Like the human aura, the aura of a tree is full of movement, with clearly defined radiation lines, showing the amount of vitality present. Flowers too are quite remarkable to watch. In fact, once you have accustomed yourself to 'seeing' the aura, the biolumines-cence of all nature will open your eyes to another world - another beautiful dimension of life.

Remember, the aura is greatly affected by the way you think, by what you eat, where you live, and also by the people with whom you associate. Your aura affects other people long before you make contact with them, and others will always have a strong sense of who you are by the atmosphere that surrounds you. You are the architect of your own destiny by the way you think, and the way you think is most definitely who you are. Think your way into a new life by creating a new and more dynamic aura ...

HOW PSYCHIC ARE YOU?

* Do you ever sense that the telephone is going to ring, and it does?
* Do you sometimes know what your partner is going to say just before they speak?
* Do you ever have strong feelings about something that is going to happen, and it does?
* Have you ever been alone in the house and suddenly felt as though someone is watching you, or standing behind you?
* Have you ever felt uncomfortable while sitting alone in a theatre or waiting in a bus queue, and when you looked over your shoulder someone was staring at you?
* Do you ever dream about specific things or situations that later happen?
* Do you ever see pinpoints of bright light around people's heads, or pinpoints of colour floating in the air?
* Have you ever seen a coloured mist around people or animals?
* Have you ever thought you have seen a shadowy figure out of the corner of your eye while you were alone in the house?
* Have you ever met someone for the first time and felt certain that you know them from somewhere, even though you don't?
* Have you ever walked into a house for the first time and immediately been overwhelmed by its warmth, coldness, happiness or sadness?
* When you are drifting into sleep do you ever hear someone call your name?
* Have you ever been overwhelmed by a fragrance that no one else can smell, and which reminds you of a dead relative or friend?
* Have you ever handled a piece of antique jewellery and found pictures and impressions forming in your mind?
* Have strong feelings ever forewarned you not to go to a certain place or do a particular thing?
* Have you ever had bad feelings about someone whom everyone

likes?

* When someone is unwell do you ever feel compelled to place your hands on them in an attempt to make them better?
* Have you ever seen the patterns on curtains or carpets change into faces?
* Have you ever been overwhelmed with the feeling that a relative or friend, living on the other side of the world, has had an accident, and you later learned that they had?
* Have you ever felt compelled to write a poem or a piece of philosophical writing which, on later examination, appears completely alien to the way you think?

It is quite common to have experienced two or perhaps three of the things listed above. However, to have experienced six or seven of them shows that you have psychic potential. If you can answer 'yes' to ten or even all the things listed, you most certainly do have a psychic skill, and so really should consider doing something about it.

I do hope my treatment of the aura has helped you.